Believe!

MW00681498

They made believers out of us — from left, Brendan Shanahan, Steve Yzerman, trainer John Wharton, Nick Lidstrom and Sergei Fedorov, taking a break between Games 2 and 3.

Credits

- Editors: **Steve Schrader and Bob Ellis**
- Designer: **Brian James**
- Photo editors: **Robert Kozloff, Robert St. John, Caroline E. Couig, Todd Winge, Alan R. Kamuda**
- Photo technician: **Kathryn Trudeau**
- Copy editors: **Ken Kraemer, Chris Clonts, Tom Panzenhagen, Karen Park and the Free Press sports desk.**
- Cover design: **Rick Nease**
- Project coordinator: **Dave Robinson**
- Sports editor: **Gene Myers**
- Front cover photo: **Julian H. Gonzalez**
- Back cover photos: **Julian H. Gonzalez**
- Special thanks: **Scott Albert, Steve Anderson, Laurie Bennett, Bob Casper, Bernie Czarniecki, Owen Davis, Laurie Delves, Craig Erlich, Thom Fladung, Chris Gee, Jennifer George, Gary Hancock, A.J. Hartley, Christine Mackey, Bill McGraw, Robert G. McGruder, Rose Anne McKean, Steven Mounteer, Brian Murphy, Jim Pesczek, Danielle Rumore, Dan Shine, Jessica Trevino, Laura Varon Brown, Erin Young.**

Detroit Free Press

**321 W. Lafayette Blvd.
Detroit, MI 48226**

**To subscribe to the Free Press, call 1-800-395-3300.
Find the Freep on the World Wide Web at www.freep.com**

Table of contents

Mitch Albom	2
Triumph and Tragedy	4
The Season	22
Round One	43
Round Two	53
Round Three	65
The Finals	81

Twice as nice

Vladdie lifts Wings to highest heights

The first one they won for the city. This one they won for their hearts. A hockey saga that began last summer in yelps of joy, and was interrupted six days later by tears of sadness, worked itself back around to joy once more, with Red Wings players in a happy mob around the net, another Stanley Cup in tow. But this one was different. It was hard-fought, it was tiring, it was long and sometimes painful. But it was always meant to be. We can see that now. What happened was less about victory than it was about belief.

MITCH ALBOM

And so, when the hockey ended, the Wings were doing what they had dreamed of doing all year long. Finally, with tears in their eyes, they handed the Stanley Cup to their fallen colleague, Vladimir Konstantinov, and that tells you all you need to know about this team. They weren't playing for themselves. They were playing for a higher cause — and it took them to the highest heights.

"TWO! TWO! TWO!" the Wings yelled as they posed for their first photo as 1998 champions, gathered around Konstantinov in his wheelchair, the Cup in his lap, a victory cigar in his hand, an unbelievable smile on his face.

"Everything we did all year, we did for this guy," Igor Larionov said. "We never stopped believing."

Believe and you can fly. Isn't that the theme of songs and stories about bravery and heroes? So here was Konstantinov, crippled in a limousine crash with team masseur Sergei Mnatsakanov six days after last year's Cup, making the trip to Washington, perhaps because he knew, in his heart, that this would be the moment. He sat all game long in Section 116 in the MCI Center, over a homemade sign that read,

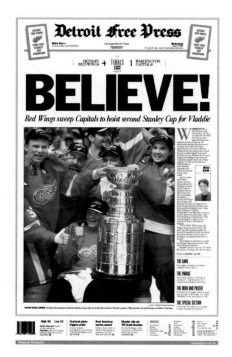

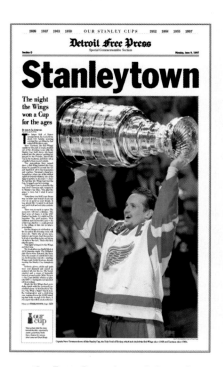

Last year, right, Steve Yzerman was alone on the Free Press' special section commemorating the Wings' first Stanley Cup in 42 years. This year, the Captain shared the front page with Vladimir Konstantinov and teammates.

"WE BELIEVE, YOU BELIEVE."

Do you believe? Konstantinov watched the first period, as Sergei Fedorov spun and drew defenders, then dished to Doug Brown, who whacked the puck past Washington's Olaf Kolzig. 1-0.

He watched the second period as Larionov dished to Martin Lapointe, who whacked a puck past Kolzig. 2-0.

He watched as Larry Murphy fired another puck past Kolzig. And as Brown put in his second of the night. He watched as Chris Osgood turned back nearly every devil's stone the Capitals fired in his direction. He watched as his former teammates dug all game long, in the corners, against the boards, in the deepest part of their hearts, to end this odyssey the way they wanted.

And finally, when the horn sounded and the scoreboard read Detroit 4, Washington 1, he watched as, one by one, they skated to him, hugged him, told him to use this to get better, maybe

the most noble use this Cup will ever see.

Believe? How could you not? The 16th victory of the postseason, played in front of No. 16?

"You know today is June 16," Steve Yzerman said, "and I remember a year ago we were sitting in Beaumont Hospital and doctors were telling us maybe Vladdie will live, maybe he'll die. And here we are one year later and he's at the arena with us, getting the Stanley Cup. I think it's been . . . it's the most emotional moment I'll ever be involved in."

Twice, nice.

DESTINY'S TEAM

What an amazing run. Before a Washington crowd that was splashed in red jerseys, before more than 19,000 watching on the big screen back in Joe Louis Arena, before all the rest of the hockey world, the Wings proved that last year was not a fluke, it was merely a start. Back-to-back Cups. Back-to-back sweeps.

But understand it. Last year the Wings were fighting 42 years of Detroit hockey demons. This year they were fighting demons of their own.

And series after series, they cut those demons down. No first-round upsets by the likes of Phoenix. No surprise attacks by the St. Louis Blues. No outhustle, outmuscle by the Dallas Stars. And no looking past the Washington Capitals.

It says something that the Wings beat such different teams with the same game: It says they weren't going to lose, no matter what you put in front of them. It says they were living for this moment: Third period, the Wings with a lead in the Stanley Cup finals, and they looked up at the big screen and there was Konstantinov rising to his feet.

"When we saw that, the whole bench became unglued," Brendan Shanahan said. "We were screaming and yelling. Scotty Bowman tried to calm us down because we still had a period of hockey to play. But there was no way. No way we were going to lose then.

"I looked down the bench and there wasn't a dry eye on the team."

One for the city. Two for the heart.

A TEAM OF WINNERS

Good things are for sharing. So beyond Konstantinov and Mnatsakanov, who was Cup No. 2 for? Where do you begin?

It was for Steve Yzerman, the captain, who last year was the symbol of a long-suffering franchise and this year was simply the symbol of excellence. His Conn Smythe Trophy as playoff MVP was a slam dunk. He led the playoffs in points, and he led the Wings in effort.

"Most fans didn't know this was the first really big trophy you've ever won," someone said to Yzerman. "Is it better when the awards come later in your career?"

"Well, I think I'd appreciate it anytime," he answered. "But it really means a lot to have the Yzerman name

on the Conn Smythe. I mean, just for my dad to know the Yzerman name is there. . . ."

He paused, choking up.

Cup Two's for you.

And it was for Chris Osgood, who all year was like a college student in line at graduation. Around him were people pondering his fate, deciding how good he could be, offering him advice. But only Osgood, ever quiet, knew what he could accomplish.

"I can't describe all the emotions I'm feeling right now," said a shaky Osgood after the Game 4 victory. "I always believed I was a good goalie."

Now you have company.

Cup Two's for you.

It was for celebrated players such as Brendan Shanahan, who fought a bad back the entire postseason — "It didn't hurt when I lifted the Cup," he joked — and Darren McCarty, who was his normal tireless self on the ice. And it was also for the grinders, such as Kirk Maltby, Doug Brown, Kris Draper, Joey Kocur and the underappreciated Martin Lapointe. These are supposedly the guys who get bloody noses, lose teeth and wear ice packs. Only this spring, they got winning goals as well.

Cup Two's for you, too.

It was for the Swedes, Nicklas Lidstrom, whose excellence we all knew about, and Tomas Holmstrom, who stunned even his coaches. Holmstrom was an end-of-the-bench man just a blink ago. Now the only disappointment in the season ending is it cuts off his amazing ascent. The way he was going, he might have been MVP in another week.

And the Cup was of course for the Russian contingent, the quiet Slava Kozlov, the cerebral Igor Larionov, and everybody's favorite millionaire, Sergei Fedorov.

It was for the "old men" on defense, Bob Rouse, Larry Murphy and Jamie Macoun. Amazingly, the latter two were late pickups off Toronto's discard pile, Murphy last year, Macoun this year. If this is how Scotty Bowman picks up discounts, he can have my Christmas list anytime.

Speaking of Bowman, this Cup was most definitely for him. The quixotic coach tied his hero, Toe Blake, with his eighth NHL championship. But for all his shouting, his crazy rules and his perplexing conversation, Bowman was touchingly human when he had to be this year, never more than before Game 3 in his brief locker-room speech marking the one-year anniversary of the June 13 limo crash. The Wings fell silent when he spoke. And when they took the ice, the series was pretty much over.

And finally, this Cup, this season, was for Slava Fetisov, "Papa Bear," the grizzled 40-year-old who might have retired had he not had one more dragon to slay, the one of memory. Remember that while the Wings all felt for Vladdie and Sergei, only Fetisov really knew what they went through. He was there, too, in the limo that awful night. Some believe that only the cushion of their bodies kept Fetisov from a crippling injury. All season, he suffered with the weight of "Why me?" — and, even worse, "Why not me?" Can you imagine questioning your own survival? Fetisov looked over more than once at his friend sitting in the stands. Maybe now his sleep will be a bit more peaceful.

"Vladdie's spirit was in our room all year," Fetisov said, kneeling next to Konstantinov in his wheelchair. "I hope this win gives Vladdie more, faster recovery."

Which is the big lesson in this whole thing, isn't it? Another Cup doesn't wash away the memory of what happened a year ago, it simply makes it a little easier to handle. Seeing Konstantinov with that trophy shows us that life goes on, that you do smile again, that the world is made up of highs and lows, and that the balance of life is that one or the other is always out there, waiting.

On this night, it was glory wrapped in victory wrapped in the tear-stained faces of a team that can skate like the wind, and a former teammate who cannot. One was for the city. Two was for the heart.

And, you know, "three" has a nice ring to it.

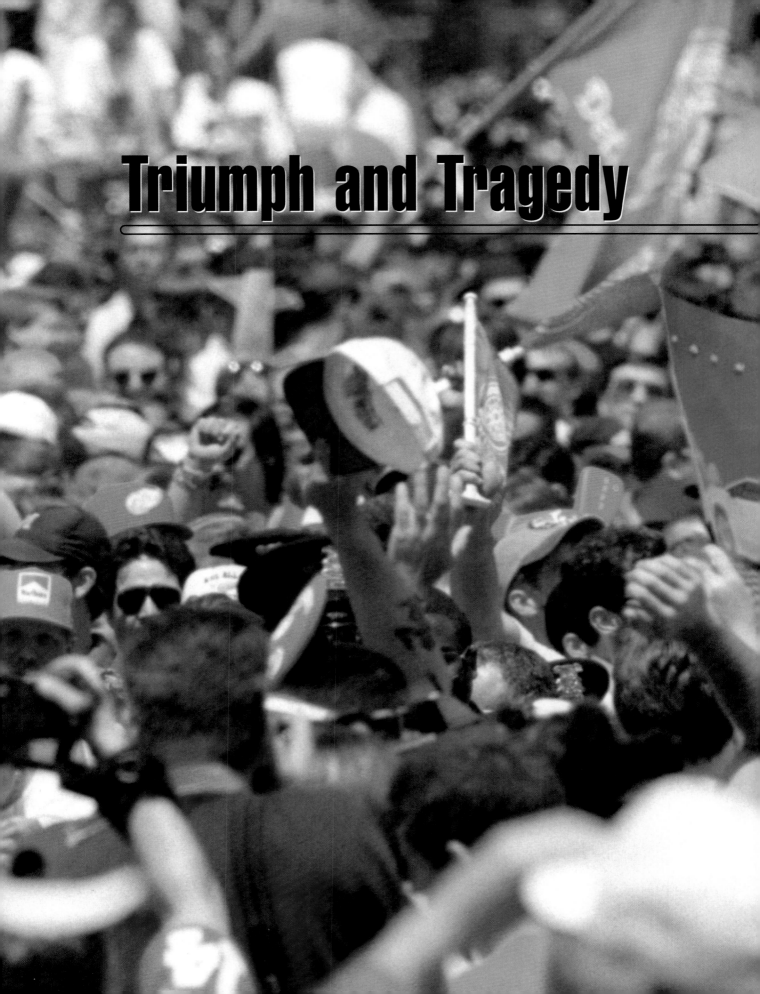

Triumph and Tragedy

Thanks a million!

Hockeytown is hookytown as fans take to the streets

Tuesday, June 10, 1997 — After a drought of 42 years, Hockeytown finally had a chance to start last summer the right way . . . by celebrating a Stanley Cup after the 1996-97 season.

A gridlock of jubilant humanity gripped Detroit's downtown streets. People painted their bodies red, wore miniature Stanley Cups and broke into cheers.

Rock music blared from normally quiet storefronts.

The Stanley Cup afterglow shone for the third day as Detroit staged a spectacular victory parade down Woodward Avenue for its Red Wings.

Police estimated up to one million people swarmed the streets to salute the Wings, who had completed their sweep of the Philadelphia Flyers at Joe Louis Arena.

The fans wore red and white, chanted and held signs offering everything from congratulations to proposals of marriage. They jammed into every square inch along the mile-long route from the Fox Theatre to Hart Plaza, pushing out along side streets far from the passage of players. They climbed trees, light poles, ladders and statues to get a better view.

Captain Steve Yzerman said the turnout stunned the players.

"We expected a lot of people here," Yzerman told the rally at Hart Plaza. "We didn't expect this. I thought nothing would top Saturday night, but

Fans began lining the parade route at 6 a.m., and by the time the Red Wings made their way down Woodward Avenue toward Hart Plaza, up to a million people had gathered. Unlike previous celebrations in Detroit and other places, the crowd behaved, and police reported no major incidents.

Sergei Fedorov brought along teenaged Anna Kournikova, a Russian-born tennis player. Although they denied being a couple, Fedorov followed Kournikova around the tennis circuit.

Instant celebrities

The Red Wings were the toasts of the town in the days following their Stanley Cup victory last summer.

Darren McCarty was at Tiger Stadium, throwing out the first pitch, Mike Vernon took his Conn Smythe Trophy on "Late Night with Conan O'Brien," and Brendan Shanahan showed off the big prize, the Cup, on "The Tonight Show with Jay Leno."

And on June 9, 1997 — two days after winning the Cup and the day before the big parade — the team attended a rally for season ticket holders at Joe Louis Arena.

The 2½-hour show was televised on Channel 50.

About 10,000 fans rocked the arena with cheers for their heroes — some of whom, they thought, might not return for an encore, such as unrestricted free agents Igor Larionov and Slava Fetisov, and Scotty Bowman, whose coaching contract was expiring.

Bowman was greeted with a standing ovation and chants of "Scot-ty! Scot-ty!" and "One more year! One more year!"

Not a bad idea, said Bowman, who ended his speech with: "We'll come back next year and do it again."

Captain Steve Yzerman was last on the stage and received the loudest applause: "Ste-vie! Ste-vie! Ste-vie!"

"In 14 years here in Detroit, I played on almost 14 different teams, it seems," Yzerman said. "This is the closest group of players, the most unselfish group of players, the hardest-working, most dedicated team I've ever been a part of."

He recalled the home opener in 1996, when rumors were swirling that Bowman was going to trade him. The fans cheered Yzerman loudly that night, too, but booed Bowman.

"Scotty Bowman's name was announced at that time as well, and his reception was a little different from mine," Yzerman said. "I think this is a great opportunity to make up for that reception."

The fans atoned, screaming for Bowman as he stood up, holding back the tears, as was Yzerman.

By Jason La Canfora

coming down Woodward was the best of all. It was the icing on the cake."

And unlike previous celebrations in Detroit and other places, the Wings' fans did their city proud. Police reported no major incidents and only one arrest — a lack of violence that started with the postgame party.

"The whole world is watching, and everyone has shown incredible class," Yzerman said. "And you should be proud of yourselves."

People began lining Woodward at 6 a.m. Wings forward Kris Draper was returning home with the Cup at 6:30 when he stopped for photos at the Spirit of Detroit statue and saw people arriving for the parade.

"Unbelievable," he said.

By 9 — nearly three hours before the parade — the crowd was a dozen deep on both sides of the street.

Downtown businesses and offices operated with thin staffs as employees poured into the streets. Restaurants and stores, which have struggled for years, were jammed on this most unusual workday.

"This is a fabulous day," associate coach Dave Lewis said. "This is a day that grandparents brought their kids who brought their children — that's what this day was all about. I don't think there was another square foot where somebody else could have been. This day was a celebration."

When the parade began, the crowd along Woodward near Michigan Avenue stood on the sidewalks. Within minutes, though, they swarmed across

The rest of the story . . .

RAISE THE ROOF

Who gets credit for last season's version of "Raise Your Hands"? Reserve goalie Kevin Hodson.

"Raise the Roof" had been around in other sports for a couple of years, but Hodson introduced it to the Red Wings when he used it to celebrate goals in dressing-room soccer games. It caught on.

"When Stevie won the Cup, he did a little 'Raise the Roof' to the guys," Hodson said of Yzerman. "It was a personal thing. Everybody knew what it meant."

Joey Kocur added: "That was the first time we were happy enough to do it in public. Guys probably wanted to do it other times but didn't have the gumption to do it. Now it's no holding back."

Hey, after winning the Stanley Cup, fans were game for anything, too. "Raise the Roof" was all the rage.

"The fans got caught up in it," Hodson said. "It's the Stanley Cup. It's 'Raise the Roof, Raise the Cup.'

"It's great when you see the fans catch on to something because that's what the Cup is all about, that's what playing is all about. The Cup is for the fans, plain and simple."

By Jason La Canfora

The Wings could raise their hands because they were sure they were the NHL's best team.

THE WHOLE TOOTH

There he was on the "Stanleytown" front of the Free Press, holding the Stanley Cup and beaming, just as he always dreamed.

Well, almost.

"Good timing, eh?" Red Wings captain Steve Yzerman said when asked about his missing upper tooth.

"Here I am, looking like a hillbilly. Not that there's anything wrong with that."

Yzerman lost the tooth two years ago, he said, but team dentist Chet Regula replaced it after a root canal. Late in the 1996-97 season, it became infected.

"I was feeling lousy all the time, and the doctor said I had a bone infection and should have it removed," Yzerman said. "After the first game against Anaheim, I finally had it taken out."

Some publications doctored photos to replace the missing tooth, and others ran photos showing only Yzerman's good side.

By Keith Gave

Before Steve Yzerman was through with the dentist, some publications doctored photos of the Wings' captain to replace his missing front tooth.

the east lanes and onto the median.

The four open lanes on southbound Woodward quickly became three. Then it was two, and finally just one lane was open.

Fans rushed the red or white Mustangs that carried the players, coaches and staff with spouses, children and friends, stealing a hand slap from their favorite players.

And hoped for more.

Trenton's Amanda Kulikowski, 19, held a sign that said: "Sergei, will you marry me?"

"He's a hot Russian!" she shouted. "I don't care that he's already married!" If she meant Fedorov, he's not — married, that is.

Goalie Mike Vernon, the playoff MVP,

held daughter Amelia. Vernon's wife, Jane, lofted a sign that read: "Thank you, Hockeytown."

Yzerman, riding with wife Lisa and their daughter Isabella, videotaped the spectacle when he wasn't holding the Cup aloft.

As the Captain approached Hart Plaza, the crowds converged around his car in a swirling mass of people, flags, brooms and signs. Police pushed through the wall of fans as the car inched toward the plaza. Yzerman's car marked the end of the parade for thousands of fans who fell in behind. A float, two bands and several parade cars — including one carrying owners Mike and Marian Ilitch — were cut off, but they eventually reached Hart Plaza.

After the rally ended about 2, the Wings headed to the Joe for a meal with family and friends, to pose for a team picture, clean out their lockers — and wax a bit nostalgic.

"I'll remember this day for the rest of my life," defenseman Nick Lidstrom said. "It was overwhelming. I hope I can experience it again. But it's a little bit sad. It's almost like a graduation in a way . . .

"It feels like you're leaving something here because you don't want it to end, but it's been a great feeling. We don't know what is coming next, we just have to enjoy it and have a great summer."

Some players began to realize that a special moment had passed.

"It's a little sad," alternate captain

Historic Detroit crowds

President Herbert Hoover, who also took in a Tigers game, drew a million people for a 1929 parade.

The Freedom Festival fireworks annually draw more than a million downtown.

More than a million people attended the parade for the Red Wings last season, Detroit police said. Here are official estimates for some other big Detroit events:

100,000
■ Dedication of the Ambassador Bridge in 1929.

125,000
■ A civil rights march in 1963.
■ The Pistons' championship parade in 1989.

200,000
■ The Pistons' NBA title parade in 1990.

300,000
■ A 1910 parade of nationwide members of the Elks.

500,000
■ The Tigers' 1935 World Series victory parade.

600,000
■ The Tigers' 1984 World Series victory parade.

1,000,000
■ The Freedom Festival annual fireworks display — if you count both sides of the Detroit River.

■ The annual Thanksgiving Day Parade, though others estimate 750,000.

■ A parade for President Herbert Hoover in 1929.

■ A parade of World War I veterans of the American Legion in 1931. The number didn't include the 100,000 who marched.

The parade crowd seemed to overwhelm the Red Wings. "We expected a lot of people here," captain Steve Yzerman told the rally at Hart Plaza. "We didn't expect this. I thought nothing would top Saturday night, but coming down Woodward was the best of all."

Brendan Shanahan said.

"That's the last time we'll get to see the fans. . . . You kind of didn't want it to end.

"I know what I've experienced and what I've felt, the flood of emotions that have come over me the last couple of days, and I'd like to hear what the other players have gone through as well before we all go our separate ways for the summer."

Ah, but the memories they would take with them.

"It's like Joey Kocur said, no matter what we do, where we go, where we live, we'll always have something that will bond us together," Darren McCarty said. "This is something, and you can't take it away."

The celebration is shattered

Limousine crash devastates team

The limo hit a tree in the median of Woodward Avenue in Birmingham. Three days earlier, the Wings had paraded down the same street in downtown Detroit.

Friday, June 13, 1997 — The team that had faced and defeated adversity all season suddenly found itself helpless, able only to watch and pray as two friends fought for their lives.

Woodward Avenue was the street on which the Red Wings paraded their triumph and shared it with a million fans in downtown Detroit.

But three days later, a few miles to the north, the euphoria that followed the Wings' 1997 Stanley Cup championship was shattered on the same street.

Defenseman Vladimir Konstantinov and team masseur Sergei Mnatsakanov were fighting for their lives after the limousine in which they were riding crashed into a tree about 9 p.m. on a median near Big Beaver Road in Birmingham. As the news came out, teammates and fans were shocked to learn that Konstantinov, 30, and Mnatsakanov, 43, were in critical condition with head injuries.

The third passenger, defenseman Slava Fetisov, 39, was in fair condition with a chest injury and a bruised lung.

As doctors worked to evaluate the injured Wings, coach Scotty Bowman, right, and associate coach Barry Smith were among those in shock awaiting news at Beaumont Hospital.

Driver Richard Gnida, 28, of Gambino's Limousine Service in Belleville, also was in fair condition.

Red Wings owner Mike Ilitch heard the news on television and rushed to the hospital about 10:45 p.m., dressed in a team windbreaker.

Trainer John Wharton arrived about 11:30, followed by captain Steve Yzerman, Brendan Shanahan, Sergei Fedorov,

---

"It's becoming clear that this is going to be a long process of healing."

Dr. James Robbins, trauma surgeon at Beaumont Hospital.

VLADIMIR KONSTANTINOV

Doctors said his head had decelerated and accelerated rapidly. He had small bruises in various places on his brain.

SERGEI MNATSAKANOV

The impact of the crash fractured his skull, causing his brain to swell dangerously.

SLAVA FETISOV

As Konstantinov and Mnatsakanov lay comatose, he was in fair condition with a chest injury and a bruised lung.

Doug Brown and Martin Lapointe. Other players followed.

The accident occurred after the men left a golf outing, one last team event before the players scattered for the summer.

Mathieu Dandenault said about 17 of the 26 Wings had been playing golf at the Orchards in Washington Township in northern Macomb County. He said Konstantinov, Fetisov and Mnatsakanov decided to leave about an hour and a half before the rest of the players, who were to reconvene at goalie Chris Osgood's home in Birmingham.

As the rest of the players were getting into their limos, Yzerman's cell phone rang with news of the accident, Dandenault said. The Captain gathered the players and let them know what had happened.

"From what Stevie said, he's fighting for his life," Dandenault said of Konstantinov. "It was the worst feeling ever."

Konstantinov and Mnatsakanov were comatose and on ventilators as doctors tried to assess their conditions, and family, teammates, friends and fans searched for signs of hope.

Dr. Karol Zakalik, who primarily concentrated on treating the head injuries, said Konstantinov's injury involved a rapid deceleration and acceleration of the head and left him with small bruises at various spots on his brain.

Mnatsakanov suffered a blow to the right side of his head, and his skull was fractured, causing swelling of the brain.

Two days after the accident — Father's Day — doctors reported the men were responding to stimuli such as light and music.

That news sent Wharton to the record store.

Russian music was played for Konstantinov and Mnatsakanov, and Queen's "We Are the Champions" — a song that was played at Joe Louis Arena after the Wings won the Stanley Cup — was played extensively for Konstantinov.

Konstantinov "does seem to respond to the voices of his teammates and his family, and these are extremely encouraging signs," Dr. James Robbins said.

He also said Konstantinov was making subtle facial expressions and hand movements. Konstantinov's wife, Irina, also told members of the Wings

The search for answers

What caused the accident?

"I might have blanked out," limousine driver Richard Gnida told police at the scene, according to Birmingham deputy chief Richard Patterson.

That seemed to jibe with Slava Fetisov's recollections of the accident.

He told friends and teammates he was seated at the glass partition behind the driver, facing Vladimir Konstantinov and Sergei Mnatsakanov at the rear of the limo.

Fetisov said the driver appeared to go to sleep and that Fetisov and the others began screaming to wake him, but the car crossed two lanes of traffic, jumped the curb and hit a tree.

"We can only assume those players and that trainer went airborne and struck ... the wall" inside the limousine, Patterson said.

Police soon discovered that Gnida had a revoked driver's license and a long list of violations, some alcohol-related.

Gnida, 28, pleaded guilty to a misdemeanor second offense of driving on a suspended license, and in November he was sentenced to nine months in jail and 200 hours of community service — helping patients with closed-head injuries.

While some experts said the sentence was harsh for the charge — Gnida admitted no responsibility for the accident — others thought the charge could have been more severe.

Officer Dave Schultz, who led the Birmingham police investigation, said prosecutors could have charged Gnida with a felony, such as driving under the

Limo driver Richard Gnida, who said he "might have blanked out," eventually pleaded guilty to driving on a suspended license.

influence of narcotics.

Schultz made the statement in "Broken Wings: The Night the Cheering Stopped," a 107-page book he wrote with Free Press columnist Charlie Vincent.

Schultz said experts determined that Gnida smoked marijuana three to six hours before the crash, but prosecutors opted for the misdemeanor charge.

"They made it look like Richard Gnida did not smoke pot that day," Schultz said. "Gorcyca's political doublespeak made it sound like he could have smoked it 30 days ago, and that's not true."

But Oakland County prosecutor David Gorcyca said no one could testify that Gnida's driving ability had been impaired.

"For (Schultz) to say we undercharged is ludicrous," Gorcyca said.

By Bill Laitner and Brian Murphy

organization that she saw her husband move his feet.

"It is important, however, that enthusiasm is tempered by recognition that these responses are somewhat inconsistent and they do not mean we expect rapid, steady improvement," Robbins said. "It's becoming clear that this

is going to be a long process of healing."

Zakalik concurred.

"We expect it will be a long time before they wake up," he said.

"Eventually they will wake up. The fact that they are not waking up today or tomorrow or in a day or two does not change my prognosis, that they will wake up."

The pet rock placed by Slava Kozlov in Konstantinov's locker summed up the hopes of the injured Wings' fans, teammates and opponents.

Hockey's family extends arms, hope

After many cheered the Cup, more pulled for the fallen Wings

Thursday, June 19, 1997 — The outpouring of joy after the Wings' Stanley Cup championship soon was overcome by an outpouring of love and concern for Vladimir Konstantinov and Sergei Mnatsakanov.

By Helene St. James

It should have been a fun night, just as his birthday party should have been fun, and the barbecues and pool parties. But the NHL awards show was a heavy-hearted affair for Red Wings defenseman Bob Rouse.

"Under any other circumstances," Rouse said. "Under any other circumstances, this would be fun. It's difficult to enjoy a barbecue, anything like that. It's always in the back of your mind. It was my birthday yesterday, I had my parents here, some neighbors over. . . .

"You think you're going to have a good time, but then you think that a couple of your brothers aren't doing too well. It's difficult to do anything."

Rouse and Larry Murphy were in Toronto to represent teammate Vladimir Konstantinov, a finalist for the Norris Trophy as best defenseman.

Konstantinov and Sergei Mnatsakanov were on the minds of many.

"It's pretty tough for those of us here not to have at least a part of you somewhere else," host Ron MacLean said. "And that's Beaumont Hospital in Detroit. Our prayers are going right to Michigan this evening."

Brian Leetch of the New York Rangers won the Norris Trophy and wished the two "a speedy recovery. We'd all love to see them around the skating rink again."

And an emotional Dominik Hasek, the Buffalo Sabres goalie who won the Vezina and Hart trophies, brought up the Wings several times.

"To Vladimir and Sergei, I want to wish them the chance to return to their families and enjoy happiness again," Hasek said. "All the best of luck to Vladdie and Sergei, we are pulling for them."

On that same night, some 750 fans prayed, lit candles and cried at a prayer vigil in Hart Plaza. "God, Please Mend Our Broken Red Wings," read one of their many signs.

Emilia Millerman, 64, of Windsor talked about signs she made in Russian for her grandchildren to take to the Stanley Cup parade. Her family emigrated from Russia 17 years ago.

She said the Russian "players said thanks at the parade for the signs and

The aftermath

The Red Wings' accident elicited an outpouring of warmth for Vladimir Konstantinov, Slava Fetisov and Sergei Mnatsakanov from around the world.

"It is so touching, so emotional," Fetisov said. "Every letter the people send me is from the heart. Especially from the kids; you can tell from their handwriting they are 6, 7, 8 years old. They send stuffed animals, usually bears, but sometimes other animals. Each letter is very special to me."

During the season, Fetisov asked the Free Press to help him respond and publish a letter to fans:

Fetisov was overwhelmed by the good wishes sent to him in the months following the crash .

Hello:

This summer, my family, friends and I went through a very tragic experience.

It helped us recover faster knowing there were people like you out there praying for a speedy recovery. My family and I would personally like to thank you from the bottom of our hearts for all your warm wishes and get-well cards.

It meant so much to my wife, Ladlena, my daughter, Anastasia, and myself that you were praying for us. We could not believe all the boxes and boxes of warm get-well cards, pictures, children's drawings, stuffed bears, guardian angel pins and so many other special things we received and are still receiving. It puts tears to our eyes when we read these touching letters. We never knew so many people really cared.

We received get-well wishes not only from Michigan, but from all over the United States, Russia, Canada and Europe. It is so nice to know that there are such loving and caring people in today's world.

I am sorry it took so long to thank everyone. I had hoped to answer each letter individually, but because of the overwhelming amount of mail I received, it is not humanly possible to do so. But I want each and every one of you to know how much it meant to my family and me. It was so thoughtful and a very special thing for you to do.

In Russia, we have a belief that when people think positive thoughts about someone, their vibes and prayers are sent to that person and help heal. I know if it wasn't for all the support and love of my family, friends and fans, I would not be where I am today.

My great friends Vladimir and Sergei love all the mail they have received. Please continue to write to them and pray for them because this really helps them with their healing process.

Your friend, Slava Fetisov

Key dates in the Wings' battles with their injuries from their June 13, 1997 limousine accident:

■ June 18: Slava Fetisov was released from Beaumont Hospital.
■ June 19: Sergei Mnatsakanov had surgery to stabilize his spinal cord after X rays discovered an injury. Still in a coma, doctors were unsure whether he was paralyzed.
■ June 24: Vladimir Konstantinov showed more consistent responses to his family and made purposeful movements.
■ June 29: Konstantinov and Mnatsakanov were upgraded from critical to serious. Vladdie had been removed from a ventilator a day earlier.
■ July 7: Mnatsakanov regained consciousness and was able to write his name in Russian.
■ July 23: Konstantinov was out of his coma but not fully awake. He was upgraded to fair condition.
■ Aug. 21: Konstantinov and Mnatsakanov were upgraded to good condition, and doctors said Vladdie was fully conscious, though not able to speak or write. Mnatsakanov spoke sentences in Russian and English.
■ Oct. 9: The Stanley Cup was taken to the hospital for a visit with Konstantinov and Mnatsakanov, hours before the Red Wings' home opener. Mnatsakanov wanted to fill it with vodka; Konstantinov was able to find his name etched on the Cup.
■ Nov. 1: Konstantinov and Mnatsakanov, in wheelchairs, visited practice at Joe Louis Arena and shared tears and laughs with teammates. "We want them to feel like they can come down here anytime they want," trainer John Wharton said, "and just be a part of this team the way they always were and the way they always will be."
■ Nov. 6: Doctors said Konstantinov had begun speaking — the names of his wife Irina, daughter Anastasia and some Russian words.
■ Nov. 9: Konstantinov left Beaumont to continue his rehabilitation in Florida during the winter months. The day before, he and Mnatsakanov received their Stanley Cup rings in a ceremony with the rest of the team.
■ Dec. 2: Doctors said Mnatsakanov, paralyzed in both legs and his left arm, would be discharged to continue rehabilitation at his Grosse Pointe Woods home.

posed for pictures with my grandchildren. They were so happy. And now this tragedy."

Fans had been holding impromptu vigils since the accident. Some made a shrine around the tree the limo hit with signs, candles, flags, cards, teddy bears, flowers and photos. The tree later was cut down after being damaged in a July storm.

Early Sunday morning after the crash, a black Cadillac pulled up to a group of people who had gathered across from the accident site.

When two men got out, the crowd was surprised to recognize one as Sergei Fedorov, said Laura Diebold, 29, of Warren. "Fedorov told us, 'I saw you guys standing there and I just had to stop. Thank you very much. We all appreciate it, and we all feel the same way you do.'"

People also began raising money for the Beaumont Foundation Closed Head Injury Fund.

For $25, fans could get their names inscribed on the 2,500-pound Stanley Cup that had sat atop the Wayne County Building and later was moved to Metro Airport.

And June 22, four days after leaving the hospital, Slava Fetisov dropped the puck for the opening face-off of the NHL & Celebrity All-Star Game at Joe Louis Arena.

Steve Yzerman, Brendan Shanahan and other Wings played in the game, which benefited the Beaumont fund and other charities.

"It's for a great cause," said Mike Ilitch Jr., son of the Wings' owner. "It's what Vladdie and Sergei would want — for us to go out and do just what we're doing."

A commitment from the heart

Wharton was always there to encourage Konstantinov

Nov. 9, 1997 — This was the day Vladimir Konstantinov would leave Detroit to continue his rehabilitation in Florida. And none would miss him more than trainer John Wharton.

By Mitch Albom

They hadn't spoken in months. Not the way most of us speak, anyhow. John Wharton never really knew what to say when he walked into the hospital room. He would take a deep breath, then grab Vladimir Konstantinov's hand and muster the meager optimism left in his heart.

"How ya doin', George?" he would blurt, using a nickname the team had for Vladdie — George, for Curious George of the children's books.

At first there was nothing. No sound. No movement. Weeks passed. The hand began to squeeze back.

More weeks passed. One day, Vladdie's eyes flickered open. No real focus. But open. Wharton got an idea.

"I have something for you, George."

The Stanley Cup was carried in. It was the first time, nurses said, that the light behind Vladdie's eyes clicked on.

"This is why you gotta keep fighting, George," Wharton whispered. "That's why your name is on this Cup. Don't stop."

Five months had passed since the limo crash that tore the heart out of this sports town and forever changed the lives of Konstantinov and team masseur Sergei Mnatsakanov.

People had gone on with their lives. There were no more vigils outside Beaumont Hospital. The Wings were into a new season. Konstantinov was ready to leave the hospital for a rehabilitation center in Florida. It's better for him there, his wife said. Warm weather. Fewer curiosity seekers.

It was a positive step. A good thing. But one man — who should have been relieved that his burden was being lightened — knew he would miss Vladdie terribly.

It was trainer John Wharton's idea to take the Stanley Cup to Konstantinov's hospital room and his idea to bring Vladdie back to Joe Louis Arena for a visit with teammates.

There is no real reason that Wharton should have tumbled so deeply into this tragedy. Sure, he's the team trainer, and so, by nature, he gets involved when players are hurt. But he has a family, too. A wife and two small children. He has his job, which is time-consuming. All good excuses for fading out of the picture.

Instead, this tragedy brought out a side of Wharton even he didn't know he had. At first, he was like all the Wings, sleeping in the waiting room, asking a million questions. But as the others slid back into their lives, Wharton kept coming. He came all summer. All fall. He came early, around breakfast, and once the season started, he came in-between morning skates and evening games.

It was Wharton's idea to bring the Cup in October. And it was Wharton's idea to bring Sergei and Vladdie down to practice.

"I had joked with Vladdie, saying, 'It's getting tough to keep coming here, why don't you come down to visit us?' And he lifted his head almost immediately and shook it. I knew he wanted to go."

Four days later, he was there, at Joe Louis Arena. He was wheeled in and seated in front of his locker, which remained untouched.

The players came by and joked and patted his shoulder. It was tough. There were tears. Seeing Konstantinov there reminded Wharton of how many times the player had come to him with injuries — "from a hangnail to a broken leg."

Now the trainer wished he could hear Vladdie complain about anything.

"There's going to be a big hole for me Monday when I go to the hospital and he's not there," Wharton said.

Isn't it funny? So many of us try to avoid burdens. But when life grabs you and throws you into someone else's, you find a reservoir of heart you didn't know you had.

Wharton planned to visit Konstantinov in Florida during the Olympic break. And maybe say, "How ya doin', George?"

And maybe Vladdie would answer, "Better."

After all, this is hockey. Don't you believe in miracles?

Cup travels to Russia, with love

Red Wings visit Red Square on mission of goodwill

Each member of the championship team gets some personal time with the Stanley Cup over the summer — to show it off for family, friends, whatever. For Slava Fetisov, Igor Larionov and Slava Kozlov, that meant taking the Cup on its first trip to Russia. "I think of it as trying to be a goodwill ambassador with the Stanley Cup," Fetisov said. "Maybe I'm wrong, but I want to see these people smiling more. Russians don't smile so often."

By Keith Gave

Sunday, Aug. 17, 1997 — A man strolling along an ancient, cobblestoned parade ground wearing a Red Wings jersey and carrying a big shiny trophy created some excitement for those visiting Lenin's tomb in Moscow.

The man walked slowly, smiling, a few friends at his side and a pack of reporters behind them.

"Oh, my God, is that Fetisov?" one tourist whispered to another.

"Yes. Yes! That's Fetisov!"

And they fell behind the pack, ignoring St. Basil's Cathedral, one of the most ornate and widely recognizable buildings in the world.

A Red Wing in Red Square. And Slava Fetisov, Russia's most famous hockey player, certainly didn't need the Stanley Cup to draw a crowd.

The reaction of Russian hockey fans to Fetisov is not unlike the way Detroiters react to Steve Yzerman: Awe, respect and joy are written all over their faces.

As Fetisov and teammates Igor

From left, Igor Larionov, Slava Fetisov and Slava Kozlov lift the Stanley Cup in Moscow's Red Square during the second day of their trip to Russia. It was the first time the Cup had been brought to Russia.

Thinking of absent friends

Even in Russia, the Red Wings' thoughts naturally were drawn to their fallen teammates back in Detroit, Vladimir Konstantinov and Sergei Mnatsakanov.

"I talked to Sergei on the phone," Slava Fetisov said, "and he was sounding pretty good. I got goose bumps and tears. I didn't know what to feel . . ."

Before Fetisov left on the momentous journey, he stopped at Beaumont Hospital for a visit.

When he told Mnatsakanov he was taking the Stanley Cup to Russia, the Red Wings' masseur had his wife go to the store for vodka for a toast.

The trip to Russia was something Konstantinov also had looked forward to, before the accident.

"We talked about it a lot after we won the Cup," Fetisov said.

"Vladdie had never been back to Russia since he left, and he was so excited about coming back."

Igor Larionov also paid a visit to the two men, taking along his daughters, Alyonka, 10, and Diana, 6.

The girls, very close to Uncle Vladdie,

While traveling around Russia, Slava Kozlov and his teammates could not help but think about Vladimir Konstantinov and Sergei Mnatsakanov, who were recovering back in Detroit.

weren't able to see Konstantinov until he was moved out of intensive care and into the hospital's rehabilitation wing.

Larionov said: "I took them in there and said, 'Vladdie, the girls are here. I want you to try to say hello to them, or at least something.' "

Konstantinov raised his hand off the bed and waved slowly.

The girls then began to sing "We are the Champions," a favorite song of Konstantinov's since the championship.

"I couldn't believe it," Larionov said. "He was moving around like he wanted to get out of the bed.

"It gave me goose bumps."

By Keith Gave

Larionov and Slava Kozlov walked around Red Square on the second day of the Russia trip, posing with the Cup near the cathedral, the Kremlin and Lenin's tomb, Russian fathers explained to sons what little they knew about the 106-year-old trophy that was being contested well before the fall of the Romanov dynasty.

Russian mothers had daughters chasing the players around seeking autographs on a picture of the Russian Five being passed around by a certain newsman from Detroit.

Excitement was written all over 8-year-old Andrei Karpov's face. Like a lot of young players in Russia, Andrei's dream had been redefined by the events of the past few days.

He was in his first year at the famous Central Red Army school that produced so many great players, including Detroit's Russian Five.

"I want to be just like Viacheslav Alexandrovich," Andrei said, referring, in the traditional Russian way of respect, to Fetisov.

And Andrei said he wanted to become a Red Army star, play in the NHL, make lots of money and drive a Mercedes. OK, so the dream might have been embellished with a bit of motherly influence, Veronica Karpova admitted.

But after witnessing history with wide-eyed awe, Andrei's dream now had a proper ending.

"I want to win the Stanley Cup," he said, "and bring it back to Red Army, just like Fetisov."

● ● ● ● ●

As Larionov looked at the Cup's itinerary in Moscow, he admitted to feeling a bit of dread about the first stop, Aug. 16 at the Central Red Army hockey school.

That meant a possible encounter with his nemesis, famed coach Viktor Tikhonov. Before Larionov left Russia, the two had feuded bitterly and publicly for years, and Larionov said they had not spoken for eight years.

Larionov wasn't looking forward to crossing paths with Tikhonov again, "but Slava told me, 'We're not going there for Tikhonov, we're going for the children.' "

He need not have worried, because the feeling was mutual. Tikhonov ducked out an hour or so before the Cup arrived.

"I can't deal with North American players," he told a guard as he left.

The Cup spent a whirlwind three days in Moscow, also visiting the Ministry of Sport, the Spartak Cup hockey tournament, the Moscow mayor's and Russian government offices and the American embassy.

It also was introduced during halftime of a soccer match at the newly renovated Luzhniki Stadium. The 62,000 in the stands included President Boris Yeltsin.

Stanleytown East hails its heroes

Kozlov, Larionov return to their hockey-hotbed home

Tuesday, Aug. 19, 1997 — The Stanley Cup had one more stop in Russia before it was passed on to Nicklas Lidstrom, Tomas Holmstrom and ex-Wing Tomas Sandstrom in Sweden — Voskresensk, hometown of Red Wings Igor Larionov and Slava Kozlov.

By Keith Gave

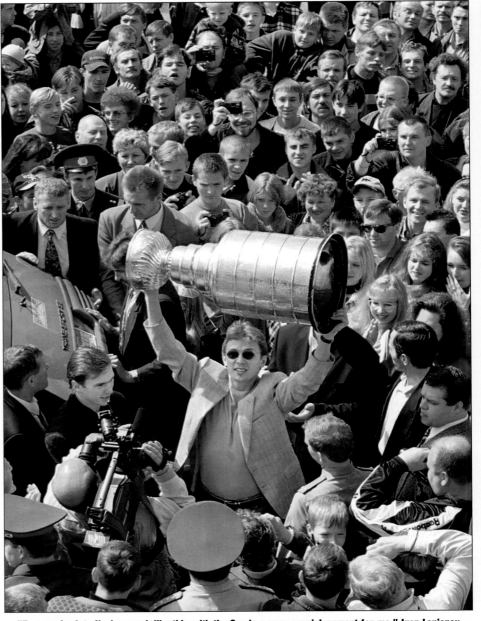

"To come back to Voskresensk like this with the Cup is a very special moment for me," Igor Larionov said of returning to his hometown. "Think about it: It's just incredible that a little industrial town like this could have such success, with such hospitality and warmth, too."

The Stanley Cup arrived for the first time in the place where the names of its sports heroes are written in silver.

And Voskresensk, a proud little city 55 miles southeast of Moscow, was bursting with pride as thousands gathered at Khimik Arena.

They cheered the most famous hero of all when he raised the Cup over his head. And when Igor Larionov brought it to his lips for the sweetest kiss of all, children serenaded him with Russian folk songs.

Larionov and Slava Kozlov, born and bred for greatness like so many others in this town built around hulking chemical plants, were honored along with Red Wings teammate Slava Fetisov.

"This is the most difficult trophy in hockey to win," Larionov told the audience of about 3,500. "It was the hardest thing for me to do in my career. But the three of us were able to bring the Cup here to our lovely city, my favorite city, Voskresensk.

"As always, we could not have done it without your support. When we played for our motherland, we always felt you there for us."

So it was for two other native sons, Colorado's Valeri Kamensky and New Jersey's Valeri Zelepukin, when their teams won the Cup. Little wonder a message in lights at one end of the arena proclaimed Voskresensk "the little place on the edge of the Earth where they play hockey as well as the best."

"You can see for yourself that this is a great hockey town," Larionov said. "And to come back to Voskresensk like this with the Cup is a very special moment for me. Think about it: It's just incredible that a little industrial town like this could have such success, with such hospitality and warmth, too."

Hundreds of youngsters, many dressed in blue-and-yellow Khimik club uniforms, posed with the Cup. Many ran their fingers across the names etched in its shiny surface.

"These are all my friends," Kozlov said. "I was born here. I played hockey here. I'm so happy to bring the Cup to my hometown. It's a special feeling right now. Look at the children. They're very happy. And I hope when they touch the Cup, they'll want to win it someday, too."

The Wings have a huge following in this city of about 60,000 because several of their games were televised last season, including all four in the finals sweep over Philadelphia.

Ask a group of 12-year-olds who their favorite player is, and the names come flying at you.

"Steve Yzerman," said Dima Solovyov.

"Fyodorov," said Andrei Nevlutov, pronouncing Sergei Fedorov's name the way Russians do.

"Larionov," Roma Krayushkin said in a most-chastising way.

After three days of lukewarm reception in Moscow, the NHL was heartened by the turnout.

Alexander Ragulin was not surprised. A defenseman for the 1972 Russian team that narrowly lost to Canada in the Superseries, he now is an official with Khimik club.

"I haven't encountered one person who has shown disinterest in this," he said. "This is a colossal event, just to witness this unprecedented visit."

Ragulin said the players should be lauded for bringing the Cup to Russia: "Igor Larionov is the first son of this town, and he's coming back.

"For him and Kozlov to get the Cup here says a lot about their attitude toward their hometown."

● ● ● ● ●

The Cup's visit to Russia was a joyous one, but not without other emotions for the three Wings.

Russian hockey is struggling with hard economic times and waning fan interest — the latter caused by the exodus of top stars to the NHL after Fetisov and Larionov helped blaze the trail.

"I have to admit, I feel a little guilty when I think about it," Fetisov said. "We opened the door, and everybody followed."

Even clubs such as Red Army play to small crowds and produce little revenue to sustain elite programs.

It's even tougher for a town like Voskresensk, hit hard by unemployment, to keep the Khimik School running at its accustomed level.

Kozlov and Larionov have sent thousands of dollars in equipment to their hometown, and Larionov financed a visit by a Khimik youth team to North America.

"The children of Voskresensk are born with hockey sticks in their hands," said Anatoly Kozlov, Slava's father and a longtime coach there.

"They love the game, especially now with the boom of hockey players going to North America. But there is so little support."

Sergei's snub

Where's Sergei? "Traveling with a friend of the family," winked one of his Russian teammates, an apparent reference to 16-year-old Russian tennis player Anna Kournikova.

Sergei Fedorov spent much of his summer on the tennis circuit, following Kournikova to tournaments such as Wimbledon and the U.S. Open.

That meant missing events such as the Stanley Cup's trip to Russia, and some of his teammates felt snubbed.

"That tells me a lot about a guy," defenseman Slava Fetisov said.

Fetisov — who helped open the door to the West for Russian players — looked upon the Cup's trip as a triumphant return, an opportunity to share the Wings' success with his homeland.

"The young guys, they make huge money, but they do not help," Fetisov said. "Everything was too easy for them. Everything was open already for them."

Fetisov suggested that Fedorov might be suffering an identity crisis.

"I understand why so many people want to become Americans," he said. "It's a very special country. But if you forget your roots, and you're not really an American and you're not a Russian anymore . . .

"This is a very special moment for us. He has to find a way to share it, even if it's just for a day."

But Fedorov rarely had been seen in the company of teammates since the Stanley Cup parade. Earlier in the summer, he also skipped an elaborate ceremony in which New York's Russian community honored their Red Wings countrymen.

These were just early indications of more trouble to come — the developing Sergei situation.

Fedorov was an unrestricted free agent, and he let it be known he expected a lucrative contract.

And if the Wings weren't willing to ante up, he might be willing to sit out the entire season and cut his ties with the team.

By Keith Gave

How I spent my summer...

Each Red Wing got some personal time with the Cup over the summer, and it traveled everywhere from Russia to the Soo. Here are some of the Cup's travels:

■ STEVE YZERMAN: "When you have that trophy around, you don't sleep a whole lot. We had a couple of parties with it; we had it out on Lake St. Clair. I think my favorite part was when we took it to Ottawa to my parents' home and invited over some of the guys I grew up playing hockey with, some of my coaches on teams I played on when I was 10 and 11 that I haven't seen in quite a while."

■ BRENDAN SHANAHAN: "My favorite memory was of a Saturday afternoon in Toronto, when I took it to my father's grave. The place was totally empty. I just sat there with it. That was my favorite moment." Shanahan's father, Donal, died of Alzheimer's disease in 1990.

■ MARTIN LAPOINTE: He took the Cup to Ville Ste. Pierre, near Montreal, where the town had a parade for him, and to a hospital to show the father of his sister's friend. Within a week, the man died of cancer. Lapointe also took the Cup to a camp for retarded children. He had pictures taken of his 16-month-old son, Guyot, "buck-naked and sitting in the Cup."

■ KIRK MALTBY: He took the Cup to the pediatrics center at a hospital and then a party for 300 people in Cambridge, Ontario. "That night, I slept with it in my bed," he said. "I had to clean it because it absolutely reeked. I don't want to tell you what time in the morning it was, but I was there with a little cloth wiping it clean. The guy who takes care of it was in bed long ago, so I had to take care of it on my own. I shined it up."

■ JOEY KOCUR: His favorite part of having the Cup was sharing it with his friends and his beer-league buddies. "Just the chance to have all my friends who've lived in Detroit all these years, waiting for a Stanley Cup, to give them a chance to drink out of it, get a picture with it. The over-30 team I played with last year at this time, they were all over. We had a team picture taken with the Stanley Cup."

By Helene St. James

The Wings opened training camp for the first time in 42 years as the defending Stanley Cup champions. "We felt pretty good about ourselves all summer," Steve Yzerman said at the Centre Ice Arena in Traverse City. "We walked around with our heads held pretty high."

Happy campers get back to work

With their championship season history, Wings prepare to defend the Cup

Tuesday, Sept. 9, 1997 — Was summer really over already? It was for the Red Wings, who banded together again for the bus ride to training camp at Traverse City. It was a chance to reflect on what they had accomplished — and on absent comrades.

By Keith Gave and Helene St. James

They were together again, the boys on the bus, and it occurred to Darren McCarty that something was all too familiar about them, yet something was quite different.

"I was just looking around at the bunch of slugs that we are," McCarty said, "and I thought, 'Geez, you know, everybody on this bus is a Stanley Cup champion.' It was pretty cool."

It got even better along northbound I-75 when someone slipped a videotape in the VCR and they watched a "Hockey Night in Canada" replay of the Red Wings' Cup-clinching 2-1 victory over Philadelphia.

"It was really the first time, since the accident really, that we've been able to sit down as a team and really take it all in together," McCarty said. "It was a great, great feeling, a special moment that I'll always remember.

"We're world champions. It's something you can't explain. There's been so much pessimism surrounding the Red Wings over the years. There's always been this dark cloud."

The Wings opened camp three months after they won the Cup and nearly three months after Vladimir Konstantinov and Sergei Mnatsakanov's limousine accident.

For the first time in years, they weren't nagged about what went wrong last season and just what they planned to do to get it right.

Captain Steve Yzerman began his 15th season no longer wondering if he would ever see the view from the top.

"We felt pretty good about ourselves all summer," Yzerman said. "We walked around with our heads held pretty high.

20   TRIUMPH AND TRAGEDY

Everywhere we went, there were congratulations and pats on the back."

But now it was history, and the Wings had to turn their attention to repeating with some notable absences — their best defenseman, Konstantinov, their playoff-MVP goaltender Mike Vernon, and Russian stars Sergei Fedorov and Slava Kozlov, who were contract holdouts when camp began.

Vernon was traded Aug. 18 to San Jose for two draft choices. His Wings career — three seasons marked by contract disputes and not-always-warm relations with fans — ended after he won the Cup, the very reason he was acquired in the first place.

But winning the Cup triggered a clause in his contract that gave him an additional season at $2 million. That was more than Detroit wanted to pay with Chris Osgood and Kevin Hodson in the wings, and the risk of losing one of them in the waiver draft.

Vernon, 34, also got what he wanted: a three-year deal worth around $2.75 million a year from the Sharks.

"I've had contract problems with the Wings since I arrived," Vernon said. "I was told that if I deliver the goods, I would get rewarded, and they weren't willing to deliver. . . . I am a little disappointed about leaving, but I have to look at my future."

The trade was the biggest move new general manager Ken Holland made over the summer, one month after his promotion from assistant GM was announced.

Holland inherited the player-personnel powers from Scotty Bowman, who signed a two-year contract to coach.

Bowman got a raise in the deal, to slightly less than $1 million a season.

"Scotty and I have talked on many occasions over the last 10 days," Holland said after the July front-office shuffle. "It's a situation we both have to be comfortable with. Now he's the head coach and I'm the GM, and it's a situation where we're both comfortable working together."

In other off-season moves, the Wings signed free agent forward Brent Gilchrist from Dallas to replace Tomas Sandstrom, who signed with Anaheim. And just before the season started, they lost Tim Taylor to Boston in the waiver draft.

Other Wings free agents — Igor Larionov, Slava Fetisov, Martin Lapointe and Joey Kocur — were in the fold before camp started, and Kozlov signed a three-year, $5.6-million deal Sept. 18.

That left only Fedorov out in the cold, still holding out when training camp closed.

Negotiations had lingered for more than a year, and the sides remained far apart: Fedorov reportedly wanted a $6-million annual salary, and the Wings had $4.5 million on the table.

More troubling, the rift seemed to be widening. Fedorov denied them, but reports began to circulate that he no longer wanted to play in Detroit.

At least some of his teammates weren't buying that.

"From things I've heard from other people, I believe he wants to be a part of this team," Brendan Shanahan said.

"There's a business aspect to this game, and it's his turn to negotiate. The team wants him back. Sergei is a huge part of our team."

Everyone wanted to touch the Cup, including these children at the Clark Park ice rink. Wings trainer John Wharton brought the Cup to Detroit's only remaining outdoor rink so that fans could touch it and take photographs with it.

Free Press awards

There was one more order of business before closing the book on the championship season: Pick the winners of the inaugural Free Press hockey awards.

A panel of experts — Freep writers Jason La Canfora and Keith Gave, Red Wings broadcasters Ken Kal and Paul Woods, former Booth Newspapers writer Len Hoyes, and Wings senior vice president Jimmy Devellano — made the following choices:

■ HOWE AWARD (named for Gordie Howe, presented to the most valuable Wing): Steve Yzerman, who transformed himself into one of the game's best two-way centers as he led the team to its first Stanley Cup in 42 years. Other nominees: Vladimir Konstantinov, Nicklas Lidstrom and Brendan Shanahan.

■ LINDSAY AWARD (named for Ted Lindsay, presented to the Wing who was a leader by word and example): Shanahan, who accepted every challenge, on and off the ice. Other nominees: Yzerman and Slava Fetisov.

■ DELVECCHIO AWARD (named for Alex Delvecchio, honors sportsmanship and gentlemanly conduct): Igor Larionov, who carries himself with grace and dignity wherever he goes. Other nominees: Lidstrom and Slava Kozlov.

■ KONSTANTINOV AWARD (named for Vladimir Konstantinov, presented to player who personifies grit and character): Konstantinov, a unanimous selection. He took on anybody, regardless of size — battling, getting knocked down, sometimes knocked out, and getting up and coming back for more.

■ AURIE-GOODFELLOW AWARD (named for Larry Aurie and Ebbie Goodfellow, presented to Wings' unsung hero): Lidstrom, one of the top five defensemen in the NHL and one of the most underrated. Other nominees: Larry Murphy, Joey Kocur, Kirk Maltby and Darren McCarty.

The Season

As the Wings' eighth Stanley Cup banner was hoisted to its home in Joe Louis Arena, the applause of captains (l-r) Brendan Shanahan, Nicklas Lidstrom and Steve Yzerman was overwhelmed by the noise of the frenzied crowd.

At last, a banner night!

Wednesday, October 8, 1997 — The Red Wings started the season with two victories on the road. Now it was time for the home opener — and a ceremony for which fans had waited 42 years.

By Mitch Albom

The sticks played taps. Twenty sticks, lightly banging a wooden applause, as the banner began to rise to the rafters. This is how hockey players show respect and admiration. Tap the sticks. Curved wood against frozen ice.

Louder now. Tap-tap-tap-tap.

Down by the Zamboni end of the rink, three Red Wings stood beside the Stanley Cup, their eyes lifted skyward. With them were two legends from the last time this franchise celebrated a championship, when Eisenhower was president and people had bomb shelters in their backyards.

Applause filled the air. Up rose the red-and-white banner — "Detroit Red Wings, 1996-97 Stanley Cup Champions." The crowd was on its feet, its noise at fever pitch. Music played. Swirling violins and royal trumpets.

Lights flashed. Horns sounded. For a moment, they all watched the ascent of their accomplishment, the players tapping their sticks, the captains, the old-timers. Finally, Steve Yzerman burst into a smile and said something to white-haired Gordie Howe.

"Thanks for coming."

The banner went higher, heading for a space just below the seven banners from earlier teams. This was fitting. It deserved a private space. What happened last June was not just another title, it was the end of a curse, a hallelujah, 42 years of thirst ended with

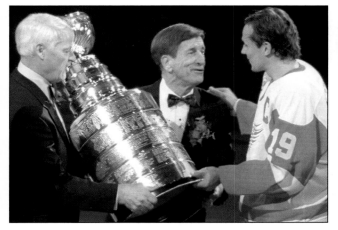

Wings legends Ted Lindsay, center, and Gordie Howe presented the Cup to legend-in-the-making Steve Yzerman, who — amid the crowd's cheers — had smiled and said "thanks for coming" to Howe.

Believe!

When Irina Konstantinov and Ylena Mnatsakanov stepped on the ice, representing their injured husbands, tears began to roll down Slava Kozlov's face.

Kozlov had talked to Sergei Mnatsakanov the night before, and he knew the Wings' massage therapist and Vladimir Konstantinov would be watching the pregame Stanley Cup banner-raising ceremonies on TV at Beaumont Hospital.

Kozlov, Slava Fetisov and Igor Larionov gave their comrades something to smile about.

Fetisov, Larionov and Kozlov did all the things the hospitalized Wings could not. With "believe" patches commemorating the wounded men on their jerseys, the trio skated, shot and scored for their friends, their brothers, in the 3-1 victory over Dallas.

Igor Larionov greeted Ylena Mnatsakanov, center, and Irina Konstantinov. Below: The patch the team wore in honor of Sergei and Vladdie.

"Sergei told me on the phone, 'I will watch you play. Play a good game,'" Kozlov said. "I'm very excited I score a goal with them watching. I think Sergei will be happy for me. I was very close to him.

"When their wives come to the ice, I think about Sergei and Vladdie very much, and I start to cry a little bit. We miss them very much. I think they're getting better."

Larionov said: "It was a very emotional night. With no No. 16 in the lineup, it was a sad moment, but we try to score a nice goal for Vladdie. . . . Vladdie and Sergei would love to have been a part of the kind of ceremonies we had tonight."

While the Wings celebrated with the banners Wednesday night, their injured friends spent the morning with the Stanley Cup, where they pointed to their freshly engraved names and drank juice from the trophy — though Mnatsakanov asked for vodka.

"Vladdie didn't want to seem to let (the Cup) go," said trainer John Wharton, who took the Cup to the hospital. "I think it's the most encouraged I've been since the accident happened. The Stanley Cup has such a tremendous ability to lift people up."

By Jason La Canfora

one satisfying gulp.

"So many times, I would look up and see those old banners and say, 'Man, it'd be nice to put one up there for ourselves,'" said Doug Brown, after the Wings had beaten Dallas, 3-1. "Now, whenever we stretch on the ice, I'll look up and see our banner. It'll be something special."

And something unique. For as the Wings got their introductions, you couldn't help but notice the numbers that were not called.

Nobody called No. 29, Mike Vernon, the playoff MVP traded to San Jose, a victim of money and age and contracts and all the other things that ruin sports for the fans.

Nobody called No. 91, Sergei Fedorov, who was without a contract, stuck in negotiations, another thing that ruins sports for fans.

And, of course, nobody called No. 16, Vladimir Konstantinov, who watched the ceremony from a hospital bed in Royal Oak, still unable to speak or walk after the limousine accident.

"Come back soon, we love you, we believe," said Mickey Redmond, the emcee for the ceremony, broadcasting a message to Konstantinov and team masseur Sergei Mnatsakanov. Konstantinov's wife, Irina, and Mnatsakanov's wife, Ylena, stepped out onto the ice with the players when the banner went up.

It was a wonderful gesture and a painful reminder. And if you don't think those two things can meld together, you haven't spent much time here this past summer.

And yet, you must believe in time, and in healing. So here was Slava

Fetisov, a guy who survived that night in the limo, taking a sweet feed from Igor Larionov and poking a shot past the Dallas goaltender, Roman Turek.

"We say that goal was for Vladdie," Larionov said. "He is very much missed. And tonight was very strange skating without him."

Something gained, something lost.

During the ceremony, Bruce Martyn, the longtime voice of the Wings, was brought out for a few words.

"Of all the things I've seen over the years," he bellowed, "nothing matched the sight of this team, in this building, holding that Cup over their heads."

The crowd roared again. It was a perfect summation. This team. This building. That Cup. These players. Those banners. Those legends. There was such a tremendous familiarity inside Joe Louis Arena that everyone seemed like old friends. There were new players, old players, new announcers, old announcers, new fans, old fans, a feel-good sea of red and white.

That's what hockey can do in the right town. This is the right town, and this is what it does: Pulls us all together, in celebration, in grief.

Thanks for coming.

"When you saw that banner raised," someone asked Gordie Howe, "did you feel that something had ended for you, because there's now a newer championship team than yours?"

"Nah," Howe said, laughing. "They still have three to go to catch us."

Well, then. Let's get started, shall we?

The return of Vernie

"It's great to look up there and know I was part of that history. ... I have those memories to cherish for the rest of my life."

Mike Vernon
on the Red Wings' championship banner

Wednesday, Oct. 29, 1997 — Look who's back. Mike Vernon made his first Joe Louis Arena appearance since he was traded to San Jose.

By Keith Gave

When we saw him last in a Red Wings uniform, Mike Vernon was chewing on a big cigar, sprawled in front of his teammates as they draped themselves around the Stanley Cup.

He had just been anointed hero of the playoffs with the Conn Smythe Trophy. He had tamed one of the most difficult jobs in sports, tending goal in a city that had become infamous for roughing up its goalies.

Tim Cheveldae and Bob Essensa were booed out of town. And a rookie was left to fend for himself behind a high-scoring, defensively inept team whose 1994 season ended in a shocking loss to San Jose.

Who can forget the tears streaming down Chris Osgood's face?

Enter Vernon, who came here with a chip on his shoulder and left with a banner in the rafters.

"That was nice to see. I liked that," Vernon said of the Wings' championship banner after a 4-3 loss to his former pals. "It's great to look up there and know I was part of that history. . . . I have those memories to cherish for the rest of my life."

And so will we. Thanks, Mike.

That's what fans at Joe Louis Arena said with applause and several handmade signs when Vernon was introduced as the Sharks' goaltender.

"It was very nice of the fans," Vernon

As the players with whom he celebrated a Stanley Cup enjoyed a goal, Mike Vernon, now a San Jose Shark, could only prepare for the next face-off.

said. "I saw those signs and I thank those fans. They've always been a class act."

Though Vernon won when it counted most, general manager Ken Holland traded him less than two months after he'd puffed on that cigar. The trade broke up perhaps the friendliest and best goaltending tandem the Wings have ever had.

Osgood played the bulk of the regular-season games the last three years; Vernon took over in the playoffs in 1995 and 1997. And the Wings followed two Presidents' Trophy seasons with a Stanley Cup.

Wednesday, in opposite nets, the former partners played gentleman hockey for two periods after what Vernon described as "the usual trash talk" before the game.

Neither held the lead for more than a few minutes until a disputed goal 45

seconds into the third period gave the Wings the lead for good.

Vernon argued that Kris Draper was in his crease when Larry Murphy scored. Officials ruled that Draper was hauled down by a defender.

And the Wings were off to their best 13-game start ever, two 5-0-1 streaks sandwiched around one loss. They did it without Vernon, Vladimir Konstantinov and Sergei Fedorov.

Osgood led the league with eight victories, had the best save percentage and the second-best goals-against average. And he did it behind a defense that was allowing far more shots and scoring chances than the previous three seasons.

It was a long way from June, but Osgood learned plenty in his apprenticeship under Vernon. Including an appreciation for fine cigars.

"I'm not going to have a bodyguard. I can take care of myself," said Claude Lemieux, left, after his second battle, above and next page, in as many seasons with Darren McCarty — who still got the best of the Avalanche defenseman.

Fists of fury fly again vs. Avs

Seconds into the game, McCarty and Lemieux mix it up

Tuesday, November 11, 1997: You know the story. On March 26 last season, Darren McCarty bloodied Colorado's Claude Lemieux as a payback for the hit-from-behind on Kris Draper in the previous playoffs. Two months later, the Red Wings beat the Stanley Cup-champion Avalanche in the conference finals. Now it was time for the first meeting of the new season, so . . . let's get ready to rumble!

By Keith Gave

The clock had ticked barely a few seconds when all semblance of time and play was suspended as sticks and gloves fell to the ice. Claude Lemieux, the man we love to hate, was re-acquainting himself with Darren McCarty, the man — let's just say he hasn't had to pay for a meal in this town since March 26, when he had Lemieux in a pool of blood on the Joe Louis Arena ice after a melee that turned this rivalry upside down.

Tuesday night, as referee Mark Faucette dropped the puck to start the game, Lemieux whacked McCarty across his chest with his right fist. A fight ensued, a real fight this time, with Lemieux squaring off instead of retreating into his shell like a turtle.

And get this: Lemieux asked for it.

He defied his coach, skated over to Colorado teammate Jeff Odgers and asked to switch positions so he could line up as a left wing, shoulder-to-shoulder with the guy who had haunted him for eight months. That's how badly Lemieux wanted a piece of McCarty.

"Are you crazy?" Odgers asked.

Of course, that has been an issue of debate since Lemieux entered the NHL 14 years ago. Crazy or not, he deserved points for courage so many have said he lacks.

"If you're going to do it, do it right off the bat," Lemieux said. "I'm not a fighter. I fight once every four or five years. I'm not going to have a bodyguard. I can take care of myself.

"We're a team, and we stick up for each other. A lot of guys last year fought when I was down. That was payback."

And it seemed to work en route to a 2-0 Colorado victory in the first of four meetings between the clubs.

"That fight right away kind of set the tone," Avs coach Marc Crawford said. "We got that out of the way and it was just great two-way hockey after that. You can say what you want about rivalries and whether fighting is good or not, but tonight it was part of it and our team really responded."

There had been talk that Lemieux was being challenged by teammates reminding him of the cruel things said about his character, not just in Detroit but around the NHL, after the events of the previous two seasons.

Nonsense, said Mike Ricci: "He had nothing to prove to us. He made that decision on his own, and as far as I'm concerned, he went above the call of duty. I think our whole team did."

Lemieux stood up to McCarty, even after McCarty reached over with his left hand to pry off his helmet and protective shield. They exchanged air punches until McCarty switched to his right, landed two jabs and then connected with a haymaker of a left hook.

And when McCarty wrestled Lemieux to the ice, there arose the loudest cheer at the Joe since a June 7 confrontation between Gary Bettman and Steve Yzerman, when the commissioner shook the captain's hand and handed him the Stanley Cup.

Colorado won the two points, but Lemieux left town with a big mouse under his right eye. Finally, it felt like hockey season, eh?

Patrick Roy, left, and Chris Osgood take center stage at center ice during their goalie title bout.

Ozzie jumps into the fray

Wednesday, April 1, 1998 — April Fools' Day . . . what an appropriate occasion for another visit by the Avalanche. This time it was a chance for Chris Osgood to earn his spurs.

By Drew Sharp

Colorado's Patrick Roy clapped his hands in delight. For the second straight year, he came to Joe Louis Arena looking to snatch a piece of a Red Wings goalie to take back to Denver and display with his other trophies.

And when the animosities between these two teams finally boiled over with a brawl near the Avalanche bench late in the third period Wednesday, Roy dropped his gloves and challenged Chris Osgood to face him at center ice, just as he did to Mike Vernon last year.

Two inches shorter and 15 pounds lighter than his adversary, Osgood didn't eagerly take the bait. He dropped one glove, perhaps hoping that Roy would go away. But he wasn't leaving.

"He did challenge me and started everything," Osgood said. "I stayed on my side of the red line. His gloves and mask were off and he was running around. To be honest, I had no idea what I was doing. I was just doing what I've seen other guys on our team do."

On the bench, associate coach Dave Lewis asked Kris Draper if the goalie could fight. "I guess we'll find out," Draper said.

And when the dust settled, Roy again found himself at the bottom of the pile, in front of the Wings' bench.

By not backing down, Osgood might have silenced any reservations about his toughness, just as Vernon did last year.

Roy "is a lot weaker than Vernie said he was," Osgood said. "The least he could do is pick on somebody his own size."

"I think (Roy) underestimated Ozzie," Draper said. "He didn't think Ozzie was going to come out, but he wasn't running away. It was good to see. . . . Roy tried to show up Ozzie, and once again it didn't work."

And the crowd agreed. Chants of "Oz-zie! Oz-zie!" reverberated throughout the building.

"It was fun to watch Ozzie go at it," Darren McCarty said. "Not too bad for somebody who's never fought before. He held his own pretty well."

And while the feud with the Avalanche continued to simmer, fans seemed to be in a forgiving mood for Sergei Fedorov, whom they had treated coolly since his holdout.

Fedorov scored both Wings goals in the third period of the 2-0 victory, giving him eight goals in 14 games.

The second score was all Fedorov. He picked off a pass at center ice, beat everyone down the ice, jumped over Sandis Ozolinsh's poke-check and beat Roy between the pads as he landed back on the ice.

The building went nuts.

"I just want to thank all the fans," Fedorov said. "I don't want to cry in front of (the media), but it was very emotional for me."

Mama's boy

One woman in the wild Joe Louis Arena crowd — the smartly dressed one who came all the way from British Columbia — didn't want to see Chris Osgood fight Patrick Roy.

That woman was Osgood's mother.

Using her son's season tickets in Section 203B, Joy Osgood couldn't believe her eyes as the pugilistic drama started to unfold on the final night of a weeklong visit.

"Chris, get back in the goal! Chris, get back in the goal!" she shouted at the top of her lungs. "No! No! No! Chris, get back in the goal!"

When the punches started, she couldn't watch. At first.

Then she stole a glance, then another. And then she started yelling at her son again. "Get him, Chris! Get him! Get him!"

When Osgood wrestled Roy to the ice near the Wings' bench, Joy started a new yell: "Oz-zie! Oz-zie! Oz-zie!"

At that point, she was just like everyone else in the stands.

The Osgood family decided to visit this week because they enjoyed seeing the Red Wings-Avalanche game last March 26, when Mike Vernon roughed up Roy.

"We knew we had to see this year's game," Joy Osgood said. "But we never expected this. … I bet Mike Vernon gives Chris a call tonight."

There was another spectator with a special interest in the proceedings.

Darren McCarty, usually in the main event of these Wings-Avs ruckuses, was an innocent bystander watching from the bench this time.

"I'm in the middle of that stuff all the time," said McCarty, who happened to be celebrating his 26th birthday. "I guess other guys wanted to do it this time. I had a good seat for it, anyway."

By Gene Myers

North America takes on the World

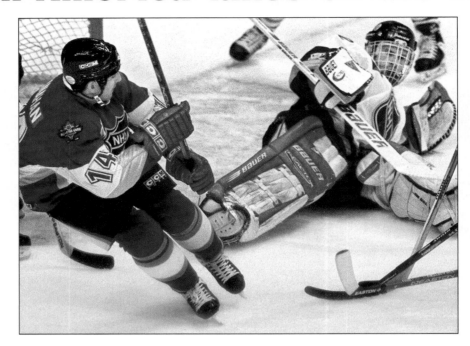

Canada's Brendan Shanahan, left, was one of four Red Wings in the All-Star Game, but the only one to play for North America. Russians Igor Larionov, who scored the game's last goal, and Slava Fetisov and Swede Nick Lidstrom were on the World All-Stars team.

Sunday, January 18, 1998 — The new All-Star Game format — North America vs. the World — was seen as something of an appetizer for the Olympics. There was a difference; this was still just for fun.

By Jason La Canfora

Red Wings center Igor Larionov and New Jersey goalie Martin Brodeur shared a moment after Sunday's All-Star Game in Vancouver.

A few minutes earlier, Larionov — the world-renowned playmaker — glided down the wing, found Brodeur overplaying the pass, and flipped the puck between the goalie's legs for the game's last score.

Larionov's World All-Stars lost to the North Americans, 8-7, in the first game of the new format, a change embraced by players on both sides.

As they lined up for the postgame handshake, the French-Canadian kid and the Russian legend shared a few words and a hearty laugh.

"He told me in handshakes he was expecting a pass from me," said Larionov, the only Wing to score. "I said, 'Hey, I shoot puck once in a while.' "

"He really surprised me," Brodeur said with a huge smile.

That camaraderie made the event special — more than just an annual collection of great goals and beautiful saves.

Wings forward Brendan Shanahan, for example, was voted a starter but didn't even notice that the New York Rangers' Wayne Gretzky was on the ice in his place at the opening face-off at GM Place.

He didn't bother to find out why he wasn't out there.

"Getting selected was enough of a thrill," Shanahan said. "It's a great format. It was more like an NHL game. There was some checking and hooking and holding."

Shanahan was the only Wing playing for North America. Slava Fetisov and Nick Lidstrom also played for the World team.

The game, and the first period alone, proved historic.

Gretzky gained sole possession of the All-Star points lead (12 goals, 10 assists); the World team scored the fastest two goals to start a game (2:15); and the first video-replay goal was scored.

Anaheim's Teemu Selanne, the Most Valuable Player with three goals, scored four minutes into the game to put the World team up, 3-0 — though play continued for several minutes until the next stoppage allowed the replay judges to discern that the puck had gone in.

Dallas Stars coach Ken Hitchcock copied Scotty Bowman a bit by constructing a Russian Four unit on the World Team.

Larionov was between countrymen Pavel Bure of Vancouver and Valeri Kamensky of Colorado, with Dallas' Sergei Zubov on the blue line with Lidstrom, a Swede. Three Finns skated together, and Lidstrom spent much time with a makeshift Swedish Four.

"I thought it was nice for the guys to play with their countrymen," Lidstrom said, "especially with the Olympics coming up."

Before it was over, Gretzky flashed back to an era when he was the most dominant individual in professional sports. He assisted on the game-winning goal by Vancouver's Mark Messier, his teammate on Edmonton's dynasties in the 1980s, that made it 8-5.

A visit with Vladdie

Konstantinov's progress rates four thumbs-up

Friday, January 16, 1998 — It was the All-Star break, and four Red Wings took advantage of the time off for a special trip to Florida. And they brought back a ray of sunshine.

By Helene St. James

As they stood close to each other, all smiles and thumbs up, Red Wings trainer John Wharton realized something was missing.

"Hey, Vladdie," he whispered, "do you want to wear my sunglasses? Do you want to take a Vladinator picture?"

The smile that lit up Vladimir Konstantinov's face was all the answer needed.

Wharton, forward Doug Brown and associate coach Dave Lewis paid an emotional visit to Konstantinov, spending an afternoon and evening at his South Florida rehabilitation center.

Coach Scotty Bowman visited the day before and took Konstantinov out for a big dinner.

"I thought he was doing very well," Bowman said. "He ate well, and he fed himself. He was laughing a lot. He ate a lot more than I did."

Konstantinov had regained the 30 pounds he lost after the limousine accident, but with less muscle.

But he had done more than gain weight. After he, Lewis, Wharton and Brown went to lunch, Wharton asked the rehab staff whether he could go for a walk with Konstantinov.

"The therapist asked Vladdie, 'Do you want to go for a walk?' and he smiled from ear to ear," Wharton said. "Next thing you know, I'm holding his left hand and the therapist is holding his right hand and Vladdie's walking completely on his own power. All we really did was balance his weight.

"He held all 195 pounds up and kept going for about 75 steps. It was emotional for us because it was way

Vladimir Konstantinov is surrounded from left by the Wings' Doug Brown, trainer John Wharton and associate coach Dave Lewis, on a visit to Konstantinov's Florida rehab center.

more than anybody expected after the accident. It's good to see that he keeps pushing through barriers and breaking through walls in his progress."

Konstantinov's speech — in Russian and English — had not progressed as quickly, but Wharton said that was common for victims of closed-head injuries.

"In talking to his therapist and people familiar with his type of injuries, that's one of the most difficult things to do," Wharton said. "He can enunciate words stronger if you force him to concentrate on it and keep it to one or two words at a time. It's going to take more time and more practice, but the capability is there."

Vague plans to bring him to

Vancouver for the All-Star Game were scrapped, but the Wings' All-Stars brought back a No. 16 World team jersey with "Konstantinov" on the back. It hangs in his locker at Joe Louis Arena.

Besides, GM Place isn't the Joe.

"When and if he makes his arena debut," Wharton said, "Vladdie and his wife want it to be at Joe Louis Arena."

Slowly, things were getting better for Konstantinov. Pictures told the story.

Bowman showed a Polaroid of Konstantinov sitting in a wheelchair, his back straight and his eyes bright and almost playful.

And he smiles even wider in Wharton's Vladinator photograph.

If you believe, you can almost hear him say, "I'll be back."

Calling on Clinton

Wings reunited with Konstantinov at White House ceremony

Friday, January 30, 1998 — As champions, the Red Wings were honored with a trip to the White House. And a reunion with a dear friend.

By Helene St. James

Their day began at 5 a.m. when Irina Konstantinov gently awoke her husband. Today is the day, she whispered to him. You are going to meet the president of the United States.

She helped him shower, she shaved him, she dressed him in a sleek, black suit. She drove him to the airport, where airline personnel waited to assist him onto the plane. And when they were seated and the plane took off, she started thinking about him.

Her Vladdie. The strapping young man she married. The man who became a star in the Soviet hockey system. The star with whom she and their daughter fled in the dead of night for an uncertain future in America.

Her Vladdie, who last season was recognized as one of the best defensemen in the NHL. A man who played such a tremendous role in the Red Wings' winning the Stanley Cup.

Her Vladdie, whose life was forever altered the night he, Slava Fetisov and Sergei Mnatsakanov were injured in a limousine wreck.

Her Vladdie, a man who now could not walk without assistance. Unable to say more than a few words at a time. Fighting to live a normal life at a South Florida rehabilitation center.

On the plane, she felt proud for him, happy for him. This trip will be tough, she thought. But he is a tough guy.

It was still early when they landed in Washington. A few hundred miles away in Detroit, the Wings were preparing to leave on their private jet.

A loose group of guys excited to meet the president, but even more thrilled to see their Vladinator.

"He looked great," center Kris Draper said after the Wings had toured the White House. "He smiled and

Captain Steve Yzerman presents a Wings jersey, with the letter "P" sewn on it, to President Bill Clinton during a ceremony honoring the Stanley Cup champions at the White House.

Konstantinov laughs after Clinton asked to take a picture with him because, "I might run for office in Russia someday."

recognized us and was so excited. It's so great to see him."

"He's been recognizing the players, and saying hello," right wing Doug Brown said. "And that's nice to see. He seems to be enjoying it."

A little later, they met President Bill Clinton in private. Coach Scotty Bowman related the first words Clinton said to Vladdie.

"He said, 'I like the look in your eyes,' " Bowman said. "And Larry Murphy said, 'You should see him when he plays.' "

About 5:15 p.m., Clinton addressed a packed crowd of players, coaches, NHL commissioner Gary Bettman, media — and plenty of politicians — in the East Room of the White House.

When he had been wheeled in by Fetisov, Vladdie smiled from ear to ear. While others spoke, he sat with Fetisov and Doug Brown standing by his side, often looking down and squeezing his shoulder.

Brendan Shanahan caught Vladdie's eye and a smile when Clinton mentioned a photo taken with Vladdie.

"I reminded him that I am term-limited in my present position," Clinton said. "And I asked him to take a picture with me. I said, 'You know, you can't ever tell, I might run for office in Russia someday.'

"So he agreed to do it. I expect it to be in the papers in Moscow any day — and I expect my popularity to soar as a result of it."

Bowman gave Clinton a miniature Stanley Cup with his name engraved on it. Then, it was Steve Yzerman's turn.

"In 15 seasons in Detroit, I've come to understand what wearing a Detroit Red Wings jersey means," Yzerman said as he clutched a white Wings jersey. "This jersey represents hard work and dedication and, once again, it represents the Stanley Cup champions."

Yzerman held up the jersey and pointed out a "P" where the captain's "C" would be. He turned it around to show off the Clinton name on the back above the No. 1.

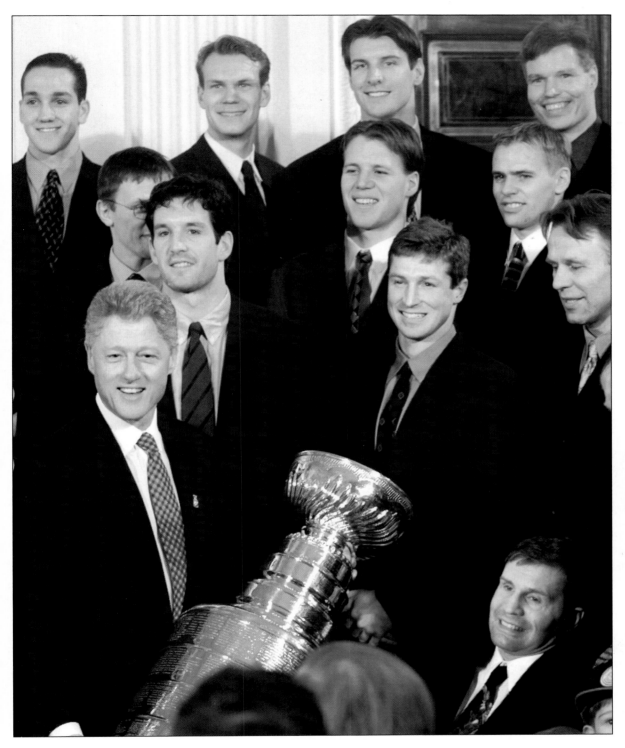

The Red Wings pose with President Bill Clinton and the Stanley Cup at the White House. "I've never gotten to hold the actual Cup before," Clinton said.

"We've even got a couple of Americans on the team," Yzerman told Clinton, who laughed.

The president thanked him for the jersey, but was even more impressed minutes later when he walked over to the real thing. The Stanley Cup.

"I've never gotten to hold the actual Cup before," the president said.

When it was over, Fetisov wheeled Vladdie back out. Irina took over, and the two headed back to the airport, to a plane ride back to their temporary home. With a memory to last a lifetime.

Her Vladdie had been a treasured guest at the White House.

"His short-term memory is not that great," she said. "So in a week he will probably forget that he was in Washington. But we have lots of pictures to remind him."

Pictures to remind them both of the day her Vladdie had the American president smiling and shaking his hand.

Like old times for Canadians

Playing for Olympic team turns into a group activity

February 8-24, 1998 — The NHL took its first winter break to send stars off to play in the Olympics in Nagano, Japan. Red Wings Nick Lidstrom played for Sweden and Sergei Fedorov — still holding out — for Russia. And Steve Yzerman and Brendan Shanahan felt like kids again playing for Canada.

By Jason La Canfora

It's a good thing the Canadians liked each other. Not only did they have to share bench space, six of them were stuffed into each room in the Olympic Village.

On the eve of Canada's first game, Red Wings forwards Steve Yzerman and Brendan Shanahan snuck down to the cafeteria for a late-night treat.

They had a taste for ice cream. No hot fudge. No cherries. Just ice cream.

"We go down to the cafeteria the night before a game for a little tradition: midnight ice cream," Shanahan said. "Eleven o'clock ice-cream breaks before we go to bed.

"We're starting to get a few more guys now. It's a different time to be in there, 11 o'clock just before bed, and you talk to a lot of athletes coming back from events."

While some athletes spent their nights partying, the Canadians were bonding around the Olympic Village, spending time with each other's families and cementing a sense of unity.

The atmosphere was similar to what the players grew up with on youth hockey teams, surrounded by parents and loved ones in the village.

"When you come out after a game and there's Mr. Brind'Amour, Mr. Yzerman and Mr. Lindros hanging out together, I think that's really helped bring us together," Shanahan said. "It's

like a tournament back in midget, hanging out in the hallways together.

"The (parents) are the ones that deserve the curfew more than the players. There's been a role reversal here. They used to be the disciplinarians, but right now, they could use a watchful eye."

In the World Cup in 1996, Team Canada wasn't as unified. There were a few cliques and, with games being played all over North America, more time was spent traveling than spending quality time together.

Players spent most days as a group. They ate together, usually three times a day, and went shopping in groups with wives and kids. Many afternoons were spent in the Canada Room at the Olympic Village, where athletes from all sports gathered to watch CBC and cheer on the other men and women wearing the Maple Leaf.

The living conditions were cozy. Six players were stuffed into small rooms, where they mingled, met others, played cards and just had a good time. It was almost like a college dorm, with a bunch of freshmen eager to meet the guys living next door.

The atmosphere was instilled on the plane from Vancouver to Japan.

The players watched a videotape of Paul Henderson's legendary goal to beat

a great Russian team in the 1972 Summit Series — a moment intrinsically tied to Canadian pride.

Their Team Canada sweaters were awaiting them in the dorm rooms, with pictures of the players in their childhood jerseys underneath. Memorabilia was strung throughout the village, reinforcing feelings of the spirit of Canadian hockey.

"We feel it's such a tradition," defenseman Al MacInnis said. "That's a word used in Canada more than anything. We talk about the commitment that (the 1972 team) had. They had 35 players on that team and obviously only 20 could play every night, and they took turns playing, and that's the kind of acceptance we needed over here.

"It's the history and the pride, and each day you think about what every Canadian is doing during the Olympics and the percentage of Canadians watching that game. You think of the other players in the NHL who would give anything to be in this situation."

So, you give 100 percent. You put team success above individual accolades. You beat the best in the world.

And if you're lucky enough to be hanging with Stevie and Shanny the night before a game, you go for a little ice cream and think about a gold medal.

Nagano a-go-go

He hit Nagano like a rock star.

Sergei Fedorov stepped off the bullet train from Tokyo wearing black jeans, a Planet Hollywood jacket from Sydney, Australia, and a poor-boy cap turned backward. Everyone, from scores of Japanese children to international journalists, took notice.

Fedorov was a late addition to the Russian Olympic team because of an injury to Alexei Kovalev. While he said he missed hockey dearly, he gave no indication his holdout would end anytime soon.

"This could be my season," he said. "This could be my season."

It didn't take Fedorov — who had been working out with the Plymouth Whalers — long to pick up where he left off. He scored Russia's first goal, 90 seconds into the opening 9-2 victory over Kazakhstan.

He finished with one goal, six points and a plus-6 rating as the Russians advanced to the gold-medal game, which they lost, 1-0, to Dominik Hasek and the Czech Republic.

Fedorov mostly declined to discuss his holdout.

But a Russian newspaper quoted him as saying he had no intention of returning to the Wings.

"I made this decision in August and still haven't changed it," he said. "They think they can break me with the help of some financial tricks, but they don't know the kind of person I am. They don't know who they are messing with."

And general manager Ken Holland said he had no intention of trading Fedorov for less than equal value. That left it to a third party to break the stalemate.

By Jason La Canfora

Still holding out on the Wings, Sergei Fedorov helped lead the Russians to the silver medal.

Red Wings captain Steve Yzerman was an alternate captain for Team Canada.

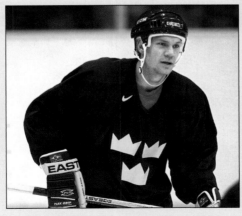

Nick Lidstrom had one goal and an assist for Sweden, which lost in the quarterfinals to Finland.

Hockeytown sent a large contingent to play in both the men's and women's tournaments in Nagano. Some highlights:

Red Wings

- SERGEI FEDOROV: Did not score in Russia's 1-0 loss to the Czech Republic in the gold-medal game. He had one goal, six points and a plus-6 rating In six games.
- NICK LIDSTROM: Had one goal, one assist and a plus-4 with Sweden (2-2), which lost in the quarterfinals to Finland, 2-1.
- BRENDAN SHANAHAN: Scored a goal in Canada's 3-2 loss to Finland in the bronze-medal game. In six games, he had two goals and was a plus-3, but missed the final attempt in the semifinal shootout loss to the Czechs.
- STEVE YZERMAN: Did not score in Canada's bronze-medal loss to the Finns. He had one goal, one assist and a plus-4 rating in six games.

U.S. men

The United States finished sixth and generally got more ink in the scandal sheets than the score sheets.

But seven of its players did have local ties: New York Islanders defenseman Bryan Berard, a former Detroit Whaler; the Hatcher brothers from Sterling Heights, Derian of the Dallas Stars and Kevin of the Pittsburgh Penguins; New York Rangers center Pat LaFontaine, who grew up in Waterford Township; Dallas center Mike Modano, of Westland and Highland; Florida Panthers goalie John Vanbiesbrouck, of Detroit; and Edmonton Oilers center Doug Weight, of Warren.

U.S. women

Three local women played big roles in the United States' winning the first women's hockey gold medal ever contested:

- LISA BROWN-MILLER: Left wing from Union Lake had one goal, three points and a plus-6 rating.
- SHELLEY LOONEY: Center from Trenton had four goals, five points and a plus-4. She scored the Golden Goal — the winner in the final against Canada, 3-1.
- ANGELA RUGGIERO: Defenseman from Harrison Township did not score but had a plus-9 rating.

Czech Republic goalie Dominik Hasek stuffs Canada's Brendan Shanahan on the final shot of the overtime shoot-out, ending the Canadians' chances for a gold medal.

Canada leaves empty-handed

Shanahan shoulders the blame for Olympic team's failure

Friday, February 20, 1998 — Canada came to Nagano on a mission to win the gold medal, and nothing else would do. But it was not to be, and afterward Brendan Shanahan felt the weight of the world on his shoulders.

By Mitch Albom

It was a hockey shot like any other hockey shot, yet it was different from anything he had ever tried. The racing of his heart told him that much.

"Take deep breaths," his friend Steve Yzerman told him. Deep breaths. He took deep breaths. Not that it would make much difference. There are rules for the rest of life, and then there are rules for moments such as this, when the world lasers down to a single unforgiving act. You are more conscious than you have ever been, you can feel your skin rising into a million bumps, and your vision is so sharp your eyes almost hurt. In these rare moments of steel-cracking pressure, the planet consists of three simple things.

You. Your task. Your heartbeat.

"Make a fake, draw him out, then go upstairs . . ." Brendan Shanahan thought as he went alone toward destiny, the puck on his stick, "deep breaths . . . deep breaths . . ."

Unlike many athletes gathered at the Winter Games in Nagano, Shanahan, 29, did not need Olympic success to build a future. He came in a multimillionaire, he would leave a multimillionaire. His income would not change if he failed at this, Canada's last chance to tie the Czech Republic in the desperation finish to a desperation game.

The winner would play for the gold medal. But with the game tied, 1-1, after 60 minutes of regulation play and 10 minutes more of overtime, the rules demanded the game come to a shoot-out, five men for one side, five men for the other, each man gets a shot on the goalie, most goals wins.

The Czech team had tried four times and put one lonely puck past the great Patrick Roy.

Canada had tried four against the great Dominik Hasek and had made none. Shanahan was the last hope.

Shanahan faked, Hasek went with him, not fooled, and the available space shrunk like a closing elevator door. Shanahan felt his heart sink even before he flicked the puck. Hasek, perfectly positioned, blocked its path.

The party was on in Prague. Czechs win, 2-1. Mighty Canada would be an also-ran.

Now, in the tunnel of the Big Hat arena, Shanahan, the pro, the multimillionaire, was wearing his team jacket and a pin his mother had sent him. He was choking back tears.

"I wanted to stick my head in the sand," he said, his voice flat, eyes dead.

But it wasn't your fault, he was reminded. Four other players didn't score either.

"I let down my team and my country," a distraught Brendan Shanahan said after he failed to score on Dominik Hasek.

"But it came down to me," he said. "The shot before me, if they scored, I wouldn't even have had the opportunity to shoot. We were all pulling for Patrick, our whole team had our hopes on him, and he pulled out the save."

He paused. "And then they open the door and ask me to go out there" . . . he swallowed . . . "and I didn't score."

Another swallow.

"And that's how I feel. . . . I let down my team and my country."

Tell me again how Dream Teams aren't supposed to care about this Olympic stuff. Tell me how it's all about endorsements. Tell me again how if you lose, you just get drunk and trash your hotel rooms.

Tell me again, and I'll show you Wayne Gretzky, struggling for words, and Eric Lindros, his eyes glassy, and Shanahan saying, "You take the hopes of all these guys out there with you. . . . You never know if you're going to be back here again . . ."

What happened was heartbreaking for Canada, but it was reaffirming for those who believe that the Olympics still represent a special kind of competition. In that frozen moment, when the gold-medal chance hung on every shot, there was not a professional on the ice. They were all children, all dreamers, there for the right reasons, for sport, for competition, to win for their country, to make a memory.

"Hero or goat," Shanahan said, "I'd stand up and ask to take that shot again.

I wanted it to be me."

It was a shot like any other shot, but it will hurt more than any he's known. It will come back vividly in the unsuspecting moments, in a dream, in a hotel room, maybe when he's alone in his car. It will hurt, it will rip a part of him he didn't know he had. And yet when Brendan Shanahan was asked whether he would come back and play in another Olympics, this is what he softly said.

"Sure . . . in a second."

The pros were supposed to dilute the Winter Games, cheapen them, maybe destroy them. Somebody forgot the awesome power of putting the world on a single stage. In the broken heart of the last man with the puck, honor was paid, and the Olympics won.

The 38-million-dollar man

Wings swallow a bitter pill to bring back Fedorov

*Wednesday, February 18, 1998 —
Sergei Fedorov said he had no intention
of upstaging the Olympics with his
contract problems. Until he signed a
monster offer sheet with Carolina.*

*By Jason La Canfora and
Helene St. James*

Sergei Fedorov
ended a 59-game
holdout, saying
to Wings owner
Mike Ilitch:
"I'm very happy
to be back, and
I will earn
every penny you
pay me."

Here's the deal Carolina put on the table for holdout Sergei Fedorov: six years, $38 million. It included a $14-million signing bonus, a $2-million annual salary and $12 million in additional, automatic bonuses. Not bad, eh?

And there was a catch, a poison pill the Hurricanes planted in hopes of scaring off the Red Wings.

The latter $12 million in bonuses would be paid in $3 million installments — but if the team made the conference finals, a lump-sum payment was due July 1.

Fedorov, a restricted free agent, signed the offer sheet. "I'm very excited," he said in Nagano. "I'm very proud this happened. Obviously, I'm eager to go and regain my life in the National Hockey League."

But where? The Wings had seven days to mull their options:
■ Match the offer, meaning Fedorov would play for them and could not be traded for a year.
■ Work out a trade with Carolina — for, say, Keith Primeau?
■ Decline to match the offer and receive the Hurricanes' next five first-round draft choices in compensation.

First the Wings explored a fourth option. Since they stood a much better chance of making the conference finals than the Hurricanes (who failed even to make the playoffs, it turned out), they thought the offer sheet was unfair.

"Certainly it's structured to try to deter the Red Wings from matching," general manager Ken Holland said.

The league agreed . . . then an arbitrator reversed that ruling, and the Wings were back on the clock.

But not for long. The Wings matched the offer as soon as the arbitrator ruled Feb. 26.

"It was an easy decision on the part of our ownership to make," Holland said. "We're a much better hockey club with Sergei."

And the team swallowed the pill with a smile, despite facing the possibility of paying Fedorov $28 million in salary and bonuses for a season in which he held out 59 games.

"The total is certainly in line with what's going on for the top players in the league," Holland said. "Certainly the difficult part is the up-front money. I'm not going to tell you it is not a tremendous amount of money. But we're looking at it over the term of the contract, the six years.

"This is the way of pro sports in the '90s. Fans may not like it because it may increase the cost of every aspect of the game. But that's the reality. If you want to win these days, this is the game you have to play."

Money aside, there also was the question of bruised feelings. Fedorov — who felt he was mistreated by the team, bounced around to a checking line and even defense — had said he no longer wanted to play in Detroit.

"I'm of the old adage, time heals all wounds," Holland said. "I've heard (trade demands) many times, and players have gone back and found a way

to make it work. I believe it's the same in this situation."

Apparently owner Mike Ilitch's checkbook and the dream of another Stanley Cup also healed all wounds, because it was business as usual the next day.

Fedorov reported to Joe Louis Arena at 8 a.m. as the Wings prepared for the Florida Panthers and their second game following the Olympic break. Slowly, his teammates began trickling in.

"The guys congratulated me about the money, and then all the joking started," Fedorov said. "At that point, it started to feel like I never left."

There also had been reports of a rift between Fedorov and his Russian teammates, who criticized him when he didn't accompany them on their Stanley Cup trip home.

"That is all in the past," Igor Larionov said. "I am looking forward and being positive. Winning the Cup, that is my concern. He is one of the best players in the world, and he will give us tremendous confidence."

Fedorov renewed one more acquaintance when Ilitch, who had undergone heart bypass surgery in January, stopped by for a pregame handshake.

"I told him there were no ill feelings," Fedorov said. "It was all business."

He said he told Ilitch, "I'm very happy to be back, and I will earn every penny you pay me. And I will be a

"The guys congratulated me about the money, and then all the joking started. At that point, it started to feel like I never left."

Sergei Fedorov
on his first day back with the Red Wings

Neither Florida's Gord Murphy nor some fans at Joe Louis welcomed Fedorov's return in the Wings' 3-1 victory over the Panthers. "I'm going to try to win all of them back," Fedorov said of the fans.

better player overall. . . .
"It was a very good handshake. We looked into each other's eyes, and everything went away."
As Fedorov expected, the fans weren't so forgiving. Some cheered, but many booed him every chance they got in the 3-1 victory over Florida.
"Everyone is entitled to their own opinion," said Fedorov, who took one shot in the game. "I'm going to try to win all of them back."

Ante up

OLD FRIENDS

When he rejoined the Wings, teammates joked that the nouveau riche Sergei Fedorov owed them dinner.

And on March 1 in Phoenix, he picked up the $10,000 dinner tab for the team and training staff at Morton's of Chicago, an upscale steakhouse. It followed a team golf outing.

"We had all day together and did a couple of things," Fedorov said. "It was nice just to get on the road and spend some time together."

OLD FOES

Was it a coincidence that the Carolina Hurricanes were owned by Pete Karmanos, a longtime rival of Wings owner Mike Ilitch?

Yep, said Karmanos, chairman of the Farmington Hills-based Compuware Corp., he was just trying to upgrade his team when he courted Fedorov. But even he never was convinced his bid would fly.

"I wasn't allowing myself to get too excited about getting Sergei in our lineup," Karmanos said.

"We put together an offer sheet that we thought gave us the best opportunity to get what we thought was one of the best players in the league, but I always assumed they would pay."

THE MILLIONAIRES

Fedorov's contract made him the second-highest-paid athlete in Detroit (average in parentheses):

- BRIAN WILLIAMS, Pistons: $45 million, seven years ($6.4 million).
- SERGEI FEDOROV, Red Wings: $38 million, six years ($6.3 million).
- BARRY SANDERS, Lions: $34.6 million, six years ($5.8 million).
- GRANT HILL, Pistons: $45 million, eight years ($5.6 million).
- SCOTT MITCHELL, Lions: $21 million, four years ($5.3 million).
- STEVE YZERMAN, Wings: $17.5 million, four years ($4.4 million).
- BOBBY HIGGINSON, Tigers: $16 million, four years ($4 million).
- BRENDAN SHANAHAN, Wings: $15.2 million, four years ($3.8 million).

Coach Scotty Bowman and the Red Wings try to regroup before their playoff opener in Phoenix. A string of injuries at the end of the regular season had cooled off the NHL's hottest team.

Limping into the playoffs

Season-ending road trip leaves fewer Wings along for the ride

Saturday, April 18, 1998 — No team was hotter than the Red Wings after the Olympic break — until they hit the last week of the season.

*By Jason La Canfora and
Helene St. James*

A healthy group of Red Wings left for a season-ending trip as the hottest team in the NHL. Riding a season-high six-game winning streak with three games left — at Phoenix, Dallas and Colorado — they seemed in great shape for the playoffs.

But they returned with key players injured and a season-high three-game losing streak.

Doug Brown scored his career-high 19th goal but suffered a separated left shoulder in a season-ending 4-3 loss to the Avalanche. The early prognosis was for him to miss seven weeks, or likely all of the playoffs.

Kris Draper also was injured, in a collision with Avs captain Joe Sakic, who lifted his knee and caught Draper above his knee, twisting it back and spraining the medial collateral ligament. He was expected to miss at least a few playoff games.

The game was meaningless, but perhaps the Avalanche was anticipating another playoff showdown with Detroit.

The Wings already were hurting with Brendan Shanahan (inflamed back) likely to miss at least the opening playoff game against Phoenix and Brent Gilchrist (out since March 5 with a groin injury) gone for the first round.

"This was by far the worst road trip, all things considered, in the eight years I've been doing this," trainer John Wharton said. "It turned out to be exactly what I hoped it wouldn't. We lost three games, we lost three guys."

And the Wings thought they were playing it safe. Even though they had a chance to catch Dallas for the No. 1 seed in the Western Conference, they decided not to play Steve Yzerman and Igor Larionov in the final three games and let them rest minor groin injuries. Yzerman stayed in Detroit with his expectant wife, Lisa.

After the rest, at least those two players were ready for the playoffs.

"I'm 100 percent sure I'll play," Larionov said. "There's no pain at all."

By this time the Wings had learned to take

Season highlights

■ STEVE YZERMAN scored 24 goals and moved into 12th place on the NHL's all-time list with 563 goals. Along the way he passed Stan Mikita, Maurice Richard, Michel Goulet, John Bucyk and Guy Lafleur.

He also tied the NHL record of Toronto's George Armstrong by going 12 straight seasons as captain of one team. During the season, Yzerman surpassed the length of Alex Delvecchio's tenure as captain of the Wings.

Yzerman also moved past Delvecchio on the team's all-time list with 846 assists. Gordie Howe leads with 1,023, and Delvecchio is third with 825.

■ LARRY MURPHY — at 37 the only Wing to play all 82 games — moved into third place on the all-time scoring list for defensemen, behind Paul Coffey and Ray Bourque.

Murphy, who scored 11 goals and 52 points, has 1,103 career points, behind Coffey's 1,473 and Bourque's 1,411.

■ CHRIS OSGOOD netted the 100th victory of his career in the Red Wings' season-opening 3-1 victory at Calgary (Osgood finished the season with 132).

With Mike Vernon traded, the microscope was on Osgood throughout the season. He played a career-high 64 games and responded with a 33-20-11 record, 2.21 goals-against average and six shutouts.

■ Two Wings got their first career hat tricks. DOUG BROWN'S came in the third period of a 5-4 victory over New Jersey on Dec. 19. KIRK MALTBY scored his hat trick eight days later in an 8-1 victory over Toronto.

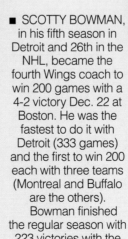

■ SCOTTY BOWMAN, in his fifth season in Detroit and 26th in the NHL, became the fourth Wings coach to win 200 games with a 4-2 victory Dec. 22 at Boston. He was the fastest to do it with Detroit (333 games) and the first to win 200 each with three teams (Montreal and Buffalo are the others).

Bowman finished the regular season with 223 victories with the Wings and an NHL-record 1,057 overall.

■ BRENDAN SHANAHAN'S output dropped off, but he still gets the award for timeliest goal.

His 28th and final goal came with 2.8 seconds left in a 3-2 victory on April 4 at Chicago. It was his team-leading ninth game-winner.

The new faces

Jamie Macoun

Dmitri Mironov

There was never any question the Red Wings could hope to replace Vladimir Konstantinov.

But when the March 24, 1998 trade deadline came around, they knew they had to bolster their defense for the playoffs.

And they did, acquiring Dmitri Mironov from Anaheim for defenseman Jamie Pushor and a fourth-round draft choice, and Jamie Macoun from Toronto for another fourth-rounder.

"We've upgraded our defense considerably," general manager Ken Holland said. "The depth allows us more options."

Mironov, 32, has a strong shot, is a deft passer and has great size (6-feet-3, 215 pounds) and reach. He has 50-point potential, especially on a team as skilled as the Wings, but said he is not overly concerned with scoring.

"I need to take care of our zone first," Mironov said. "And if I get a chance to jump up in the play, I take it. I'm here to play the way the coaches tell me to play. Scoring a lot of points, that's not my job, actually."

The downside? Mironov was eligible for unrestricted free agency after the season.

"Certainly, we paid a steep price by trading Jamie," Holland said. "If we advance far in the playoffs, it's worth it."

Pushor, 25, was Detroit's second-round pick in 1991 and spent his entire career in the organization. Leaving wasn't easy.

"I worked hard, I played hard and I worked hard off the ice," Pushor said. "Sometimes your best isn't good enough. I've been kind of preparing myself for it, because I knew something was going to happen."

Macoun, 36, came from the Maple Leafs, who threw the Wings a plum in Larry Murphy for virtually nothing at the trade deadline in 1997.

Macoun, a stay-at-home defenseman, plays a rough, abrasive game and is a noted character guy who won a Stanley Cup with Calgary in 1989.

By Jason La Canfora

---

adversity in stride anyway, with Scotty Bowman guiding the way.

"At the beginning of the season, everybody was being negative about the team because we were missing some key guys," Larionov said. "But he found a way to balance the team, and that says a lot about his wisdom. Players know he knows the game.

"This year was special. It was not easy to have the kind of tragedies as we had here and keep playing the way we did. It's easy to say we have so much talent on the team, so it's easy to work with this team. But sometimes you can have a lot of superstars and the team does not do well."

Despite the loss of Vladimir Konstantinov and Sergei Fedorov's 59-game holdout, the Wings finished 44-23-15 for 103 points, a nine-point improvement over their Stanley Cup-winning season.

Bowman did it by cultivating a balanced attack that scored 250 goals — second to St. Louis — without a player among the NHL's top 20 scorers.

The stars sacrificed ice time to spread the wealth, and 11 Wings finished in double figures in goal-scoring.

Shanahan led the team with 28 goals. Even with the lockout season of '95, it was the first time since 1981-82 the Wings failed to produce a 30-goal scorer.

And other than the lockout season, Yzerman's 69 points were the lowest total to lead the team since '81-82.

The Wings' resiliency was clear from the beginning; their 10-1-2 start was their best ever. They had only three losing "streaks," twice losing two in a row before finishing the season with the three road losses.

But right before that closing slump, the Wings had won a season-high six in a row. Their 13-5-3 record was the best in the NHL after the Olympic break, and they had gone 12-4-2 since Fedorov's return.

So the Red Wings seemed poised for a run at the Stars' two-point lead. But they blew a third-period lead and lost, 2-1, at Phoenix on April 14.

The Stars clinched the title the next night with a 3-1 home victory over the Wings. Detroit's season-ending 4-3 loss at Colorado added injury to the insult.

The Wings went into the playoffs seeded third and with Phoenix as a first-round opponent. The Stars were first and the Avalanche second because of its Pacific Division title (the Avs had the fourth-best record in the West).

Dallas won its first Presidents' Trophy for the NHL's best regular-season record, but . . .

"It's all about championships," Stars coach Ken Hitchcock said. "We all chase Detroit and we all chase Colorado until somebody knocks those guys out. . . .

"Doesn't matter how many points you finish ahead of them, you're still chasing."

Chris Osgood allowed three goals, but that didn't matter because Grind Liners Joey Kocur (two goals) and Darren McCarty, below, roughed up the Coyotes in a 6-3 victory.

Wings win, and everything's Kocur

Wednesday, April 22, 1998 —
So it was back to the playoff
grind for the Red Wings —
and the grinders were quite
ready to regain the magic.

ROUND ONE
GAME ONE

By Mitch Albom

don't want to give the folks in Phoenix early indigestion, but when Joey Kocur scores two goals on your team, you'd better check your diet.

Yes, I know it's only the first game of the playoffs. Yes, I know some teams need time to get loose. But two goals — by Joey Kocur?

Here was a game in which Detroit, not Phoenix, was decimated by injuries to Brendan Shanahan, Kris Draper and Doug Brown. Yet the Red Wings lit up Phoenix like stars in a desert sky.

Two goals? Joey Kocur? Yep. And once, he even used his stick.

"The first one, I really didn't know it went in until I heard the fans," Kocur said after the Wings' 6-3 victory. "To be honest, I didn't even know if it was going to be allowed."

It was early, first period, when Kocur flew into the crease and tried to hit the brakes before he slammed into goalie Nikolai Khabibulin. Kocur

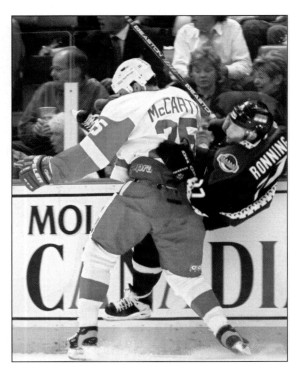

stopped in a spray of ice. As he did, the puck hit his skate and went in.

His other score was more legit; Kocur used his stick for this one, a second-period blast past Khabibulin. Not-so-jolly Nik — who also gave up goals to Nick Lidstrom and Darren McCarty — had seen enough and headed for the showers after 36 minutes. His replacement, Jimmy Waite, quickly gave up a goal to Kirk Maltby for a 6-1 Wings lead.

"This game went the way you draw up an opener," McCarty said. "Of course, usually it doesn't work the way you draw it up."

What a nice kickoff to a long postseason. And maybe Kocur offered a harbinger of things to come. His last playoff goal came in the first game of last year's finals against Philadelphia — and look how those worked out.

"How's it feel to be the Wings' leading scorer in the playoffs so far?" he was asked.

Kocur laughed. "I'm going to savor this day."

There has always been something very Detroit about Kocur. He's an original bruiser, who goes back to the rough-and-tumble years, when Nick Polano, Harry Neale and Brad Park took turns coaching and the playoffs were an annual exercise in futility.

Last year, Kocur, 33, his knuckles scarred from years of fighting, thought his career was over. Having bounced to several teams, and having won a Stanley Cup with the New York Rangers, he was playing in beer leagues.

The Wings gave him a second life. He responded by tapping into — and occasionally socking into — the roots of this team, a quiet symbol of power.

"Do you know the last time you scored a goal?" he was asked.

"Last year," he said, "Dec. 31."

"Were you worried you might go 0-for-1998?"

"Nah," he said, "I still had the first few months of next season."

The Red Wings' own Karen Newman proves she can do more than sing "The Star-Spangled Banner" as she flies from the Joe Louis rafters to save Al the Octopus.

Our hero: Newman!

In her five years as the Red Wings' anthem singer, Karen Newman's renditions of "The Star-Spangled Banner" have occasionally rattled the Joe Louis Arena rafters.

Never did she envision jumping from them on a rescue mission.

But, hey, the playoffs require everyone to give a little extra.

The stunt — unveiled during the pregame hoopla for the playoff opener with Phoenix — started with a video on the scoreboard.

Al the Octopus was being held prisoner, and only Newman could save him, the plot went. And she did, surprising fans when she swooped down from the rafters to the ice, suspended on a cable.

A grand entrance, eh?

"The only thing is, I have to jump off this platform," she said. "I never thought five years ago that I'd ever be flying from the rafters down across the ice. It was pretty nerve-racking."

After landing, Newman, dressed in black, disappeared through the Zamboni gate and returned in a red-sequined dress to sing the anthem.

"I had to do a complete costume change in two minutes — which itself is pretty amazing, because it takes me an hour to get dressed in the morning," she said.

The journey started routinely enough, with an elevator ride to the fifth floor of the arena.

"From there, I'm escorted across a maze of catwalks over the ice to the area where I launch off," she said. "I get harnessed in, but the scary part is I have to climb over a railing and get on a two-foot platform — with nothing else between me and the bottom of the Joe. I'm all clicked in and safe, but that's where I have to stay until I get my cue to launch and go."

On cue, Newman, 65 feet above the ice, took a breath, stepped into space and trusted the equipment.

"We had three runs the day before," she said. "The first one was terrifying. . . . I said I was game to try it, but I didn't know how high up I was going to be. The lighting guys were betting I wouldn't do it. I think I closed my eyes the first time."

When she landed on her first game-day performance, Newman turned and raised her arms to each side of the arena while two attendants released her from the harness.

"The crowd went nuts," she said. "When I got down to a level where they could recognize who I was, I think they were shocked it was actually me. I think they were really excited by it."

By Matt Fiorito

Coyotes bite back

Friday, April 24, 1998 — It looked like the Red Wings had picked up right where they left off last season. Then they had to play Game 2 against Phoenix.

By Jason La Canfora

Phoenix pummeled the Wings and Tomas Holmstrom, who earned his first career playoff point. Below, Coyotes Jeremy Roenick and Gerald Diduck celebrate their victory.

Momentum doesn't have much of a shelf life in the playoffs. Give it about two days — the 48 hours between games. Each contest is its own season. Plots rarely carry over. New heroes emerge and grab our attention. Anything can happen.

The Red Wings handled Phoenix with such ease in Game 1 that it was difficult not to expect a short series. But one game later, everything changed.

The Wings played sloppy and inept defense in Game 2, yielding more goals than they had in any game all season, including two on shorthanded breakaways. They committed numerous turnovers and were beaten to pucks.

All the damage the Wings did to Phoenix in the playoff opener was shoved right back at them in a 7-4 loss at Joe Louis Arena, and the underdog Coyotes had a new playoff life as they headed home with the series tied at 1.

The Wings, who had won six straight playoff games dating to last spring's Stanley Cup run, gave up four goals in the second period, then tried desperately to recover.

"Too many turnovers," Darren McCarty said. "We didn't play well at all defensively. That's something we take pride in, and we didn't do it tonight."

The Coyotes led, 2-1, on first-period goals by Mike Gartner and Keith Tkachuk; Igor Larionov scored for the Wings.

Rick Tocchet scored less than five minutes into the second, then Jeremy Roenick took over with his shorthanded tallies.

Roenick, who had four points, stripped Larry Murphy at the blue line and beat Chris Osgood to his glove hand. About six minutes later, Dmitri Mironov put the puck on Roenick's stick at center ice and it was 5-1 Phoenix with 7:36 left in the period.

The teams combined for two more goals in the next 27 seconds.

Mathieu Dandenault scored eight seconds after Roenick's goal. Dandenault, Tomas Holmstrom and Anders Eriksson got their first career playoff points on the goal.

Nineteen seconds later, Tkachuk scored his second with bodies scrambling in front. Sergei Fedorov capped the scoring in the six-goal second period and Detroit trailed, 6-3.

Tocchet and Fedorov each netted his second of the night in the third.

There's no doubt it was a team loss, but the target of much of the criticism was Osgood, who allowed seven goals on the first 18 shots and admitted, "The second period didn't exactly go the way I wanted."

But his teammates weren't pointing fingers in the goalie's direction.

"We hung Ozzie out to dry," McCarty said. "It's not fair. He's got breakaways on him, or a 50-goal scorer all alone in front of him. It's our fault.

"And when he finally does make a save, you hear the fans clap sarcastically. That's not right."

It turns out to be a short flight

Sunday, April 26, 1998 — As expected, the Red Wings came out flying as the series shifted to Phoenix. It lasted about a minute.

By Jason La Canfora

The Red Wings couldn't have scripted a better start — or a worse finish.

And if fans had any doubts — about Chris Osgood's ability to lead the Wings in the playoffs, the impact of the loss of Vladimir Konstantinov, and the team's chances of repeating — they intensified on this day.

Sixty-one seconds into the game, it didn't seem possible.

Sergei Fedorov scored on a breakaway with the game's first shot. Thirty-one seconds later, Brendan Shanahan, who had missed the first two games with a sore back, banged in a rebound.

Two shots, two goals. Two shifts, two goals.

But the Wings wasted opportunities to expand the two-goal lead that lasted into the third period. Then they watched fans in America West Arena go wild as Phoenix came back for a 3-2 victory that gave the Coyotes a 2-1 series lead.

"We didn't play the game we wanted to play when we were up," Osgood said. "We have to win the next game. It's as simple as that."

The Wings, who entered the game 36-2-3 when leading after two periods, were starting to realize they had a problem with their power play. The Coyotes, 21st in penalty-killing in the regular season, had stopped 19 of 22 power plays in the first three games, including two crucial five-on-three situations.

A goal on any of Detroit's first five power plays might have done in the Coyotes. A goal late in the second period, with the Wings on a long two-man advantage, might have changed the tenor of the series.

"Obviously, a power-play goal would have been the difference," Larry Murphy said. "The biggest problem was we got up two goals, and we just sat on

Chris Osgood couldn't bear to watch after being pulled for a sixth attacker during the 3-2 loss at Phoenix.

it. We never really took the play to them after that."

Darren McCarty picked up a roughing penalty as the second period expired, and the Coyotes' Rick Tocchet did what the Wings failed to do: Take advantage of a game-altering opportunity. Oleg Tverdovsky's shot came high at the throat of Osgood, who tried to glove it. Instead, he yielded a rebound and Tocchet popped it in.

A minute later, Igor Larionov dumped a Coyote in front of the net and Phoenix cashed in again.

Jeremy Roenick fired low from the blue line and Osgood failed to handle the puck. It struck his glove, fell gently, caught a piece of his leg and rolled inside the post. The game was tied at 2 with 17:41 left.

"I could handle that shot 10 times and not have it come off me that way," Osgood said. "Instead, it spins into the net."

Roenick wasn't through.

Phoenix won a face-off. Tverdovsky (three assists) fluttered the puck high, where — with five bodies converging in front — it caught Roenick's elbow and deflected above Osgood's glove with 7:13 left.

"I was still really confident we were going to win the game," Osgood said. "Usually, when that happens to us, we pick things up."

Before this game, the Wings were 35-1 in games in which they gained a two-goal lead.

The Coyotes didn't seem to care.

Martin Lapointe and the Wings were down, but not out, as they peppered Phoenix reserve goalie Jimmy Waite in their 4-2 series-tying victory.

No reason to Waite

Tuesday, April 28, 1998 — They're all must-win games in the playoffs, Brendan Shanahan said. Especially when a loss would mean a 3-1 deficit.

ROUND ONE
GAME FOUR

By Jason La Canfora

It took breaks to win the Stanley Cup in 1997. And the breaks began falling the Red Wings' way again in Game 4 with Phoenix at raucous America West Arena.

The Wings fell behind early, had a goal disallowed, then conjured up some of their own good fortune in a 4-2 victory that tied the series at 2.

The Wings got some timely bounces, watched Coyotes goalie Nikolai Khabibulin leave a tight game with a groin injury, and scored a goal with almost no time left in the second period.

The Wings owned the third period, and Nick Lidstrom sent the Phoenix fans home early when he batted down a clearing attempt in the neutral zone and blasted it past Jimmy Waite for a 4-1 lead with about six minutes left.

Shane Doan scored for the Coyotes at 18:31.

"I thought we played our system a lot better, and I thought we were a lot more aggressive on the puck," Lidstrom said. "When we dumped the puck, we had guys going to chase it down, and I thought that was the difference compared to the first three games. We put a lot more pressure on them."

Not at first. The Coyotes started out with more intensity and took a 1-0 lead midway through the first period when a Rick Tocchet shot deflected in off Chris Osgood's skate.

It was the Coyotes' fourth power-play goal in their last 10 chances and Tocchet's fifth goal of the playoffs.

The Wings' luck changed 3:22 into the second, when Brendan Shanahan threw the puck on goal. It hit Khabibulin and bounced right to Igor Larionov, who scored on a backhander while darting to the crease.

Then Tomas Holmstrom — who was caught with his foot in the crease on Sergei Fedorov's apparent goal late in the first period — sent the puck behind the Phoenix goal, where Fedorov was skating full-speed. Fedorov fed Slava Kozlov cutting to the net, and the Wings led, 2-1.

Adding to the Coyotes' woes, Khabibulin left with a groin injury with nearly 30 minutes left, and Waite replaced him.

Break No. 2 for the Wings came as the second period ended.

Shanahan sent the puck from the corner, and Jamie Macoun — with 75 goals in more than 1,000 career games, and none this season — knocked it in for a 3-1 lead as the final tenths-of-a-second ticked off.

Feeling better

The Red Wings started the playoffs already behind their remarkably injury-free pace of 1997, but things were looking up by Game 4.

Kris Draper was back after sitting out the first three games with a sprained knee. So was Martin Lapointe, who missed one game with a hamstring injury.

"It was a big emotional boost for everybody in the locker room to get them back," associate coach Dave Lewis said. "Those two guys mean so much to the team, and they probably don't get the recognition they deserve. They brought energy to the locker room before the game even started. As we got going, it got even better and better."

Brendan Shanahan (back) and Brent Gilchrist (groin) also played in their second games after missing two, giving the Wings four strong lines. Gilchrist had missed the final six weeks of the regular season.

And Doug Brown was making a speedier-than-expected recovery from a separated left shoulder and was due to begin skating soon.

The back was still a sore point for Shanahan, and he took exception when Mike Stapleton cross-checked him in Game 4. Shanahan returned the favor and took a match penalty with less than five seconds left.

That meant an automatic league review, but the NHL did not suspend Shanahan for Game 5.

The news wasn't so good for the Coyotes, who already were missing top defenseman Teppo Numminen since Game 1 with a groin injury.

They left goalie Nikolai Khabibulin in Phoenix when the team traveled to Detroit for Game 5. He left Game 4 midway through the second period with a groin injury.

By Jason La Canfora

The right combination

The revamped Sergei Fedorov line scored all three Wings goals in a 3-1 victory, one each by Fedorov, Slava Kozlov and Tomas Holmstrom.

Thursday, April 30, 1998 — New heroes emerge every year in the playoffs. This time it was Tomas Holmstrom's turn as the series returned to Detroit.

By Jason La Canfora

They are two-thirds unrestrained creativity, one-third dogged obedience; two-thirds finesse, one-third brawn; two-thirds Russian, one-third Swedish.

One scored his 103rd career playoff point, one behind Alex Delvecchio for No. 3 in team history. One became the eighth Red Wing to surpass 25 career playoff goals.

The other scored his first career playoff goal in his sixth game.

Sergei Fedorov, Slava Kozlov and Tomas Holmstrom bullied and baffled Phoenix in Game 5 at Joe Louis Arena, helping Detroit win, 3-1, and take a 3-2 series lead.

The new line combination accounted for all three Wings goals, each scoring one.

"I said we did it with these lines last year and it worked, let's get back to last year," coach Scotty Bowman said. "Sergei and Kozzie had to get back together, and we don't have Dougie Brown, and Homer (Holmstrom) deserves the opportunity."

Simple as that. They harassed backup goalie Jimmy Waite from the drop of the puck.

Kozlov, second on the Wings with eight playoff goals last spring, slid behind the Phoenix defense but caught a post 90 seconds into the game. He was a demon, pestering and threatening at the same time. Holmstrom was a rock, absorbing abuse as well as giving it.

While driving hard to the slot, Holmstrom was sent flying to the side of the goal by a check. He shrugged it off and hustled back to his spot atop the crease. Kozlov swiped the puck from a Coyote at the blue line and whipped it toward the goal. Holmstrom was alone for the deflection, his first career playoff goal, and the Red Wings led, 1-0, nine minutes into the game.

The Wings had produced 11 shots in

11 minutes, but Coyotes forward Rick Tocchet staved off a rout by scoring on a rebound, tying the game at 1.

But Kozlov wasn't finished.

Anders Eriksson wove a cross-ice pass near center ice, catching three Coyotes flat-footed.

As they bounced into one another, Kozlov beat Waite with a perfect shot to the glove side, just under the crossbar, for a 2-1 lead.

"That was Kozzie's patented roofer," Darren McCarty said.

More genius followed 67 seconds into the second period.

Holmstrom worked the boards and punched a break-out pass ahead, and Fedorov beat everyone to the puck. Gerald Diduck dropped to the ice as Fedorov faked a shot, edged to his left and fired below Waite for one of the prettiest goals of the playoffs.

"There's only a half-dozen players in the league that you'd want to pay to see alone," Bowman said.

"And he's one of them. He'll reach his prime now."

Captain Steve Yzerman drew first blood in the Wings' 5-2 series-clinching victory in Phoenix.

Quieting the Coyotes

Sunday, May 3, 1998 — The Red Wings had learned in recent years that the first round was a survival test, even for the best. And they passed in Game 6 at Phoenix.

By Mitch Albom

Since the days of the Bible, man has come to the desert looking for a sign. Sometimes it's a burning bush. Sometimes it's two stone tablets. And sometimes it's a puck that ricochets into the net off the back of a goalie's skate and silences 16,000 howling fans.

A first-round Stanley Cup series that took six games, 12 days — and felt like forever — finally was over. The Red Wings advanced on a hot afternoon when the penalty box was busier than the women's rest room.

Typical of the series, it was a day of bumps, bruises, the constant howling of the white-clad Phoenix fans, and an endless stream of penalties, most of them on the Coyotes.

Still, the result remained in doubt until late in the second period, when Sergei Fedorov sent a clearing pass along the boards with 1:37 left.

The puck skidded along the boards, then, inexplicably, bounced out, as if smacking an invisible wall. It hit goalie Jimmy Waite in the back of his left skate and slid into the net for a 4-2 Wings lead.

Waite, looking the other way, had no idea what happened. He was standing up when the puck struck. As the crowd moaned, he sprawled into a butterfly, more out of instinct than anything. Too late.

"Most of the time, I wouldn't want to score like that in a playoff game," Fedorov said after the Wings won, 5-2. "It really isn't fair to the opponent."

But he's not going to give it back.

Fedorov's little miracle broke the spirit of the Coyotes. From that point, they played like a team bent on trying, not winning. And when the final horn sounded, the Wings took their bumps, bruises and benevolent bounces and headed home happy.

"Sergei's goal," Brendan Shanahan said, "was a nice break."

Right. And "Exodus" was a nice book.

"As defending Stanley Cup champions," someone asked Steve Yzerman, "is winning the first round a sense of relief?"

"In a way," he said. "But the last few years, it's

Phoenix goalie Jimmy Waite learned you can't tempt fate. Sergei Fedorov's fluke goal with 1:37 left in the second period deflated the Coyotes, giving the Wings a two-goal lead.

always been an upset if we lose in the first round."

Which is what makes what the Wings did here significant. This was more than defeating a .500 team. It was surviving the land mines of the first round, which claimed Stanley Cup runner-up Philadelphia, Eastern Conference champion New Jersey and archrival Colorado.

"I think what's happening is, at the end of the regular season, the six, seven and eight seeds are all in a dogfight to make the playoffs, while the top teams are kind of coasting in," Yzerman said.

"Then, when the playoffs start, those lower-seeded teams already have been working hard, and they get a jump."

Many things went right for the Wings this day. They ended an 0-for-17 slump with four power-play goals on nine chances, including two by Shanahan and one by Yzerman. Fedorov, Shanahan, Yzerman and Nick Lidstrom all had three-point games.

Brent Gilchrist, who returned from a long injury layoff in Game 3, became the 13th Wing to score a goal in the series. Chris Osgood was strong as the Wings killed off a five-on-three Coyotes power

play for 1:34.

But it was fitting that the nail in the coffin came from Fedorov's stick, also on the power play. You can't say enough about how he played in this series. His six goals were twice the total of his next closest teammate. And even when other guys scored, he seemed to have done something — an assist, a setup, a steal, a deceptive spin — that lit the wick for the explosion.

"Sergei can play anywhere," Scotty Bowman said.

And to think he almost played somewhere else.

Round Two

Slava Fetisov wasn't invited to the Blues' celebration of Todd Gill's shorthanded goal. Steve Yzerman questioned the officiating after St. Louis' 4-2 victory. "We didn't play a great game, but you'd expect better officiating than that," he said.

Whistle plays the Blues' tune

ROUND TWO
GAME ONE

Friday, May 8, 1998 — Surprise! Anticipated second-round opponent Colorado was upset by Edmonton. Instead, the Red Wings drew St. Louis, well-rested after a first-round sweep of Los Angeles.

By Jason La Canfora

Red Wings coach Scotty Bowman and his associate coaches, Barry Smith and Dave Lewis, stood on an empty bench, looking stunned.

The second period had just ended tied at 1, but St. Louis would open the third period with nearly two minutes of a two-man advantage.

Lewis stormed to the dressing room. A water bottle came flying to the ice from the bench after Steve Yzerman

headed to the box for high-sticking 11 seconds after Brent Gilchrist was penalized for hooking when Jim Campbell seemed to take a dive.

The Blues' power play, their best weapon, had a double-barreled opportunity, and they capitalized for a 4-2 victory and a 1-0 series lead, even though star Al MacInnis missed the game with a groin injury.

"Some of those calls were a mystery," said Yzerman, who was whistled three times. "But we did take a couple of bad penalties. We got sloppy and made

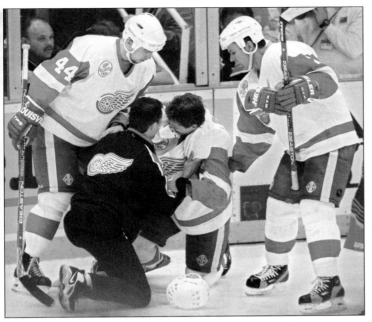

Wings trainer John Wharton attends to Igor Larionov, who was slashed by Chris Pronger in the third period. Larionov required 15 stitches to close the wound to his right ear.

Yap! Yap! Yap!

Sometimes, Martin Lapointe can't suppress the urge to yap.

Such as when he battled with huge St. Louis defenseman Chris Pronger in the corner, burst to the front of the net to trade blows with Rudy Poeschek, then deflected Igor Larionov's shot past Grant Fuhr to tie the game.

The red light was flashing, the crowd was standing, and Lapointe snapped his neck to glare at Pronger and began an expletive-laced tirade in the big guy's face.

This was less than 35 minutes into the series. The Blues might not have been Colorado, but it was just the start of the verbal hostilities among the teams' top trash-talkers.

"They're talking and yapping at our top players, and sometimes I get caught up in that mode," Lapointe said. "I think it keeps the emotions up and keeps me in the game."

But even yappers have a code: What's said on the ice, stays on the ice.

Lapointe confessed to chiding Pronger about his frequent use of his stick, but only in vague terms: "He uses his stick a lot, and sometimes I tell him, 'What would you do without the stick?' Just stuff like that."

Joey Kocur said there also is a method to the mouthiness.

"If somebody is thinking about something else, even for a split second, it takes their mind off the game," Kocur said. "That's what it is. You're trying to get someone to think about something other than what they should be thinking about.

"If you can do that, you've accomplished something." Pronger isn't a shy sort, either.

"Prongs can dish it out, and he can take it," Blues teammate Craig Conroy said. "He likes to talk, and when he's playing, he gets under their skin. They're yapping to Prongs, and Prongs is yapping right back."

True devotees consider yapping an art form. And it helps to have a witty guy such as Brendan Shanahan, who might be able to dish some dirt on his former teammates.

"You might be able to find out something that most guys wouldn't know," Kirk Maltby said. "So you kind of hold it in your arsenal until there's a good chance to use it."

Blues tough guy Kelly Chase fancies himself as being handy with his punches and punch lines. Though he would rate Kocur and Shanahan his trash-talking equals, he wouldn't extend the same status to Lapointe.

"I can't understand Lapointe," Chase said. "I'm sure he's saying something. Marty's got a lot to say. I don't know if any of it is witty.

"Darren McCarty's got some good lines in on me once in a while, and I understand Maltby might have some good wit to him."

Shanahan often chides Chase about the infrequency of his shifts. Chase recalls laying three solid one-liners on Shanahan recently, only to suffer a knockout blow later.

"He wanted to laugh at my lines, but he just didn't want to say anything right then," Chase said. "Then there was a TV time-out, and I was just kind of skating around, and he looked at me and goes, 'You don't get credit for minutes played being out here now.' "

By Jason La Canfora

mistakes that we don't usually commit."

St. Louis capitalized on the opportunity when Campbell banged in a rebound 18 seconds into the third period as he and Brett Hull battled Nick Lidstrom in front.

Coming into the series, the Wings had two main concerns about the Blues: goalie Grant Fuhr and St. Louis' potent power play.

But Campbell's goal was the only time the Blues would score with the man-advantage, even though they had eight chances.

When everyone in red and white expected Kerry Fraser to atone for the call, nothing happened — even when Blues captain Chris Pronger whacked Igor Larionov in the head with his stick moments after Campbell scored.

Larionov required 15 stitches to close the wound to his right ear, but Pronger was not penalized.

"One of the guys who saw it on the replay said it looked like a deliberate act to whack Igor," defenseman Jamie Macoun said. "The referee appeared to be at a great vantage point to see it.

"Accidents are accidents, but some of them are penalties."

The Blues took a two-goal lead when Pierre Turgeon sent a pass to the slot from behind the net, and Hull whacked the bouncing puck in with 16:12 left to play.

Campbell made it 4-1 by smacking a rebound high past Chris Osgood at 10:28, and the Wings' Tomas Holmstrom cut it to 4-2 with a power-play goal with 3:14 left.

The teams had traded first-period goals: Todd Gill's shorthanded goal on the Blues' first shot and Martin Lapointe's deflection of a Larionov shot.

Bowman, who has clashed with officials before and picked up fines along the way, refused to criticize Fraser.

"I never have any problem with the officiating because I have nothing to do with it," Bowman said coyly.

Yzerman wasn't so reticent.

"We didn't play a great game, but you'd expect better officiating than that," he said. "The officiating wasn't good. It was awful."

Brutal game, momentary horror

Sunday, May 10, 1998 — Down 1-0 in the series, Game 2 was crucial to the Red Wings. But an injury to an opponent put it all in perspective.

By Mitch Albom

Chris Pronger is as big as they come. He is 6 feet, 5 inches tall, with a beefy frame, pounds of muscle and an impish face that says if you want the rough stuff, that's fine by me. With his front teeth out, he is the picture of the schoolyard bully, a Goliath on skates.

But a little piece of rubber felled Goliath. It began as an 85-m.p.h. shot off the stick of Dmitri Mironov and ended like a bullet, landing square in Pronger's chest, just below his heart.

ROUND TWO
GAME TWO

The Blues captain doubled over. He tried to skate away, took a few steps, then fell flat, a redwood dropping in a forest. Players waved frantically for the trainers. Pronger was on his back, his eyes open in ghostly fashion, vacant from the inside.

Everybody's touchable. Big guys, small guys, everybody. The trainers raced out and immediately checked Pronger's pulse. It was falling.

"DO SOMETHING!" players yelled.

The trainers cut open his jersey, fearing his heart was in spasm and they would need to revive him with CPR. When the jersey peeled away, several players recoiled in shock.

"He had a red mark the size of a puck on his skin," recalled Detroit trainer John Wharton.

Wharton and the St. Louis medical staff crouched around the 23-year-old defenseman, ready for the worst. Then, suddenly, he snapped back. His heart resumed its rhythm, his eyes returned from the outer limits. He mumbled, "My parents are in the stands. . . . Tell them I'm OK."

They put him on a stretcher and wheeled him to an ambulance. The lights went on, and the ambulance sped to the hospital.

Tomas Holmstrom was swarmed after he scored in the second period. The Wings blew open a 1-1 tie by scoring three goals in the second period, handing St. Louis its first loss in the playoffs.

Everybody's touchable.

This would prove to be the theme on a brutal afternoon at Joe Louis Arena, from the life-and-death lessons that Pronger offered, to the less significant overtones of the actual game, a 6-1 victory for the Wings.

"I think everyone was rattled after the things with Chris," Brendan Shanahan said. "When the PA announcer calls for his mother to come down from the stands, and here it is, Mother's Day, well, it sheds a lot of perspective on the sport."

The sport — and the puck. The little black object of desire can be the most lethal weapon in the game.

"I was thinking about that kid in

Martin Lapointe was one of the Wings' hardest hitters throughout the playoffs, to which the Blues' Scott Pellerin could atest.

A remarkable recovery

While players, coaches and fans feared for his life, Blues defenseman Chris Pronger soon had another concern: Would he be allowed to play in Game 3 in St. Louis?

Pronger was rushed to Henry Ford Hospital and recovered quickly after being felled by Dmitri Mironov's shot in Game 2. But he was kept overnight for observation while the team returned to St. Louis.

"He is fine," said Blues team doctor William Birenbaum. "He is talking, his blood pressure is fine, and all the tests so far are fine. Everything's normal."

Doctors determined that Pronger went into cardiac arrhythmia, an irregular heartbeat, for nearly a half-minute after he collapsed on the ice.

Birenbaum said, "His heart rhythm was a little bit slow and irregular, but he came to right away and was very talkative. During the ride in the ambulance, his bio signs were stable at that point. He wanted his parents to know that he was OK."

Pronger was released from Henry Ford Hospital the next morning, departing with his father, Jim, and Blues general manager Larry Pleau. They rushed to a waiting car and were whisked off to Metro Airport, where a private plane awaited.

In St. Louis later that day, Pronger underwent a thorough cardiac examination, including an electrocardiogram, which gauges the rhythm of the heartbeat, and an echocardiogram, which provides a three-dimensional look at the heart to help determine structural damage.

The Blues captain was determined to play in Game 3, especially with fellow defenseman Al MacInnis' status still uncertain after missing the first two games with a groin injury.

Nine hours before face-off, Pronger walked into the St. Louis dressing room for the first time since the incident, but he was still hooked up to a portable electrocardiogram.

Tests revealed no structural damage to Pronger's heart, but doctors still wanted to watch him skate and shoot for nearly 20 minutes a couple of hours before the game.

Then, after another examination, they cleared him to play. Pronger took the Kiel Center ice — with MacInnis, who also returned — to a thunderous ovation. Even Wings fans in attendance paid their respects.

Pronger took the hoopla in stride, calling it "just another playoff game. . . . Put everything behind you. Just go all out and play 100 percent and let the chips fall where they may."

By Drew Sharp and Helene St. James

Chris Pronger collapsed after being hit just below the heart by an 85-m.p.h. shot from Dmitri Mironov.

western Canada who got hit in the chest and died," Wings captain Steve Yzerman said. "I've seen guys hit in the head, hit in the throat. When you think about it, it's a surprise we don't get hit more often."

Later, St. Louis forward Terry Yake took a slap shot in the head, went down and grabbed at his helmet as if it were crushing his skull.

"I could feel it swelling underneath," said Yake, who scored the Blues' goal. There was a bump the size of a golf ball on his forehead, topped by blood-soaked stitches.

Pronger's momentary horror — early in the third period — sucked the life out of the game.

"None of our players liked to see what happened," Wings coach Scotty Bowman said. "Every player feels the same way; they're pulling for each other. It took a lot out of the game, that's for sure."

But the outcome had already been determined, thanks to three second-period goals by Nick Lidstrom, Yzerman and Tomas Holmstrom that busted open a 1-1 tie. This St. Louis team, which had not lost a game in the playoffs, had now lost one. Its invulnerability was gone.

Everybody's touchable.

Proving that was the Wings' first

objective. The Blues had been scar-free in the playoffs. Five victories, no losses. A team gets used to that. A team rolls on that. A team swells with confidence on that.

The Blues had not scored fewer than two goals or surrendered more than three in the playoffs.

That all changed.

The series is tied, 1-1. Remember, these things are novels. Lots of twists and turns.

The theme in Game 2 was how even the seemingly untouchable can be wounded. Pronger and the Blues will be back for more.

Darren McCarty went flying into the net over Grant Fuhr, and so did Al MacInnis' 90-foot slap shot past Chris Osgood.

Rattled? Not by a long shot

ROUND TWO
GAME THREE

Tuesday, May 12, 1998 — The series shifted to St. Louis for Game 3. And afterward, Red Wings fans could say, "All's well that ends well."

By Jason La Canfora

He saw the puck all the way.

Chris Osgood was in position as St. Louis' Al MacInnis wound up from center ice and spanked a low, 90-foot drive that skimmed the ice. Osgood was down, his glove hand ready. No traffic in front. The puck just got through.

With 54.4 seconds left in regulation and the score tied at 2, the puck found the tiniest cranny between Osgood's glove, armpit and chest.

Everything Osgood worked for the past six games — his strong play since giving up a soft goal in the first round against Phoenix amid the pressure of replacing Mike Vernon — seemed lost in the frustration that enveloped him as he shifted from post to post and stared up-ice.

But two hours later he saw Brendan Shanahan slide the puck through Grant Fuhr with 8:48 left in the second overtime for a 3-2 Red Wings victory at the Kiel Center and a 2-1 series lead.

"If it was a breakaway, I might have gotten down in a fetal position on the ice and sucked my thumb," Shanahan said. "I didn't even have time to think."

While half of the Wings mobbed Shanahan, the other half rushed to Osgood's side.

"Chris needed it," Martin Lapointe said. "He knew that he made a mistake earlier, but he also needed to know that he did a great job. And if it wasn't for him making some big stops in overtime, we wouldn't have had the chance for Shanny to win it."

But Osgood wasn't whipping himself for MacInnis' goal.

"It's your guys' responsibility to be downers," he told reporters. "I just put it out of my mind as soon as it happened and I told myself: 'We'll just have to do this the hard way.' I can't allow myself to think: 'Damn, what happens if I give up the next goal?' I hadn't lost any faith in myself.

"It wasn't a physical error, it was more or less mental. . . . I learned something tonight."

Before MacInnis' sixth goal in six games against Osgood this season, the Wings goalie had a 1.84 goals-against average and .929 save percentage during the past 358 minutes.

"You can see the composure and character Chris has and this hockey team has," Darren McCarty said. "The chatter in the room before OT was, 'No big deal, no big deal. We're not going to let it get us down.' We knew we were going to keep taking it to them."

The Wings dominated the first OT but endured the biggest scare.

Blues forward Craig Conroy beat Osgood to his stick side with 10:11 left in the first OT. The puck smacked the far post, slid along the goal line and appeared to go in, with Osgood reaching back.

Conroy gestured to the goal judge, celebrating his goal that never was. Both posts had given the Wings new life.

"I knew it didn't go in," Osgood said.

The Blues and their fans were charged from the get-go. They were

Larry Murphy and Igor Larionov congratulate Brendan Shanahan, who came to Chris Osgood's rescue with 8:48 left in the second overtime.

playing at home for the first time in three weeks, and defensemen MacInnis and Chris Pronger were in the lineup together for the first time this series.

The raucousness diffused when McCarty scored 3:10 into the game. MacInnis, taking his first shot of the series, tied it with a blistering slapper on the power play.

The Blues rode that goal and the home crowd the rest of the period but lost the lead in the second when Todd Gill's clearing pass hit a skate and led to Tomas Holmstrom's third goal in three

games on a wrist shot while alone in the slot.

The victory seemed in place. The Blues went minutes without shots and were booed by the same fans so eager to cheer them earlier.

Many of the fans were in their cars listening on the radio when MacInnis did the improbable, and those who remained went nuts.

Some returned to watch 30 more minutes of hockey, and then went to their cars wishing they had never come back.

Nick has the knack

By Helene St. James

Slava Fetisov, one of the greatest defensemen ever, called Nick Lidstrom "the brightest star among the new generation of defensemen."

And, Fetisov said, that was not nearly enough praise.

Should Lidstrom want more, he need look no farther than the list of top vote-getters for the Norris Trophy as the league's top defenseman.

Lidstrom was one of three finalists announced by the Professional Hockey Writers Association, with St. Louis' Chris Pronger and Los Angeles' Rob Blake. The winner was to be named in late June at the awards banquet in Toronto.

Typically, the modest Lidstrom downplayed the nomination.

"I'm really honored to be nominated," he said. "It's nice to get the recognition, but really, right now I'm focusing on the playoffs."

The voting was conducted at the end of the regular season, when Lidstrom led all defensemen with 59 points in 80 games.

But Lidstrom's value goes deeper than points. When the Wings lost Vladimir Konstantinov, a Norris finalist last season, the pressure on Lidstrom grew exponentially.

"People thought we wouldn't have a chance when we lost Vladdie," Lidstrom said. "But everyone stepped up to make up for Vladdie's loss. It's not just about me. This is a very deep and talented team."

Teammates put Lidstrom right at the top of that list.

"Nick was the MVP of our team this year," forward Brendan Shanahan said. "I'd take six Nick Lidstroms on defense any day. You'd be set for life. There's nobody in the league that's dominated at both ends of the ice this year like he has."

Perhaps Lidstrom's greatest strength is his puck sense, sort of a sixth sense of reading a play and positioning himself to pounce on a loose puck.

"Yeah, and when he does get one, he does the right things with it," St. Louis coach Joel Quenneville said. "He's just got that knack, be it anticipation or puck sense, of positioning."

Lidstrom is one of the NHL's best one-on-one defensemen. He is not big — a slender 6-feet-2, 190 pounds — and doesn't throw thunderous body checks. But rarely does he get beaten, because he is so good with his stick, using it to push opponents' sticks and arms to fight for the puck.

"Pretty much every time I stepped onto the ice," the Blues' Brett Hull said of Lidstrom, "he and Larry Murphy were out there, and I rarely saw any room to operate. Both are tremendous position defensemen.

Brendan Shanahan, on Nick Lidstrom (above): "Nick was the MVP of our team this year. I'd take six Nick Lidstroms on defense any day."

"I wish he was bigger and more inclined to go after you. That way it would be easier to make a move on him or to get him to bite. You just can't rattle him into making mistakes."

The quiet Lidstrom did drop one bombshell this season. After playing with the Swedish Olympic team in Nagano, he said he might return to his homeland when his Wings contract expires after the 1998-99 season.

Returning to Sweden "is still an option," he said, "but it's something that my family and I decided not to talk about until after the playoffs.

"Afterward, we'll sit down and seriously look at what's best for us. But it's not about money. And it's not about being unhappy here, because I'm not."

There's no keeping 'em down

Thursday, May 14, 1998 — Game 4 was in St. Louis, and the Red Wings weren't about to pass up a chance to take a stranglehold on the series.

By Jason La Canfora

Just when it appears the Red Wings are on the verge of being whipped, when they seem most vulnerable, they are deadly.

When road games are tied on blasts from center ice, or the opposition scores a tying goal in the final seconds of a period — no problem.

The same resolve that produced a double-overtime Game 3 victory after Al MacInnis' 90-foot shot shocked Hockeytown was evident again in the Wings' 5-2 victory over St. Louis at the Kiel Center.

Detroit took control of the second-round series, 3-1, with a chance to clinch at Joe Louis Arena.

"This was very similar to the double-OT game, and we had to respond," associate coach Barry Smith said. "There's a lot of character in this room. They talked about it, and then they went out and did it."

ROUND TWO
GAME FOUR

After jumping to a 2-0 lead, the Wings headed to the dressing room tied after allowing a goal by Pierre Turgeon with 6.4 seconds left in the second period.

Again, they took the play to St. Louis when the puck was dropped for the third period, and again Sergei Fedorov emerged as a star, with two goals and an assist.

Fedorov retrieved the puck behind the goal with Blues defenseman Chris Pronger draped over him, as he had been all game. Pronger knocked Fedorov on his backside in the corner, but even from the seat of his pants, Fedorov managed to pass the puck to Tomas Holmstrom.

With virtually every Blue drawn to the right side, Holmstrom found Slava Kozlov cross-ice. Kozlov made it 3-2 – 72 seconds into the period.

Had Fedorov ever practiced such an unlikely pass?

"Practice?" he said. "How can you practice sitting down and going backwards and making pass? Is not usual, is it?"

About six minutes later, Steve Duchesne couldn't handle a pass on the point. Kris Draper pounced on it and made a perfect feed to Fedorov, who beat Grant Fuhr on the shorthanded breakaway for a 4-2 lead.

Fedorov ended the evening with an empty-net goal, and the Blues faced the daunting task of winning three in a row, including two at the Joe.

"This is one of the lowest moments I've had in quite awhile," Blues defenseman Duchesne said. "It wasn't too long ago that we were actually leading this series, but that now seems like ages ago."

Brendan Shanahan, who ended Game 3 in double OT, gave Detroit its first lead, off a feed from Igor Larionov.

Shanahan was almost behind the net when he shot

Brendan Shanahan, above, and Sergei Fedorov (two goals and an assist) peppered Grant Fuhr in salting away a 5-2 victory.

near-side and beat Fuhr with the type of improbable angle goals he has made famous. Less than 10 minutes in, St. Louis was trailing, 1-0, for the second straight game.

Fifty-four seconds into the second period, it was 2-0. Fedorov's stick got tangled with Duchesne near center ice, and Draper sprang Joey Kocur for a breakaway. Kocur finished it with a low shot for his third goal of the playoffs.

But 22 seconds later, St. Louis' Jim Campbell got to the low slot and poked in a rebound, making it 2-1 with the Blues' first goal in more than 53 minutes.

The Blues closed the period with another rush, and the building erupted. Craig Conroy fed Turgeon, who switched to his forehand at the last second and tied the game at 2.

Momentum had seemed to shift. The fans were going crazy, and the speakers pumped. Everyone, it seemed, was too high. Everyone, that is, except the Wings.

"Oh, we get rattled," Wings captain Steve Yzerman said, "but we just continue to play."

Blues not willing to go quietly

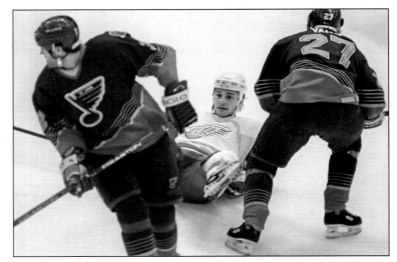

Sergei Fedorov gets flattened by Mike Eastwood, left, and Terry Yake. He and the rest of the Wings couldn't get off the mat to avoid a Game 6.

Sunday, May 17, 1998 — The last time the Blues saw the Kiel Center, they were booed off the ice. But they came to Joe Louis Arena desperate for a return trip to St. Louis.

By Drew Sharp

Though they didn't win control of the series, the St. Louis Blues won something that is perhaps equally important when you're fighting for your playoff life — respect.

"I guess everybody's going to have to hold off on those plane reservations to Dallas," Craig Conroy said. "After all that I was reading and hearing, I guess some people thought we wouldn't even show up today. But we'll see you guys back in St. Louis."

Who would have figured?

The Red Wings are notorious for denying opponents that last gasp of air once they have them by the throat. But in a 3-1 Game 5 loss, they played as if they expected the Blues to suffocate themselves.

The night before, the Stars eliminated Edmonton in five games and advanced to the Western Conference finals. "We let them up off the mat, and you can't do that to a veteran team like St. Louis," Brendan Shanahan said.

The Blues were a much more confident team.

"Maybe some thought that we would just roll over and quit, considering how we struggled at home the last two games," Geoff Courtnall said.

The Blues took advantage of laziness in the Wings' defensive zone and deposited two straight shots past Chris Osgood early in the second period. And when Todd Gill's blast from the point deflected off a Wing's stick to give the Blues a stunning 3-0 advantage — in the second period — the Ozzie detractors in the stands emerged once again.

But this was a team collapse.

"Today was our worst game so far of the series," Osgood said. "Less than our best effort isn't going to work against a team like St. Louis."

Less than best? Choose your adjective for the Wings' effort — undisciplined, reckless, cocky?

"Sloppy is a good word," Steve Yzerman said. "We tried to get a little too fancy in our own end, and we kept giving up the puck. They played smart and patiently. All we've done is make it more difficult for ourselves, and we've given them a big boost."

Perhaps the biggest boost went to someone who probably figured he didn't have anything to prove in an already illustrious career — goalie Grant Fuhr.

Fuhr's 35-year-old body has been stitched together repeatedly in recent years, and his reflexes had seemed a hair too slow in the series. But on this day, he made 29 saves, allowing only Martin Lapointe's second-period goal.

"That was the Fuhrsie that we've all come to expect," Conroy said.

A previously passive Chris Pronger also returned to the living. A week after his heart scare, Pronger was his normal, agitating self. "We're alive," Pronger said. "We lived long enough to go back to St. Louis, and that's all we were looking for."

Grant Fuhr made 29 saves. "That was the Fuhrsie that we've all come to expect," teammate Craig Conroy said.

Takin' care of business

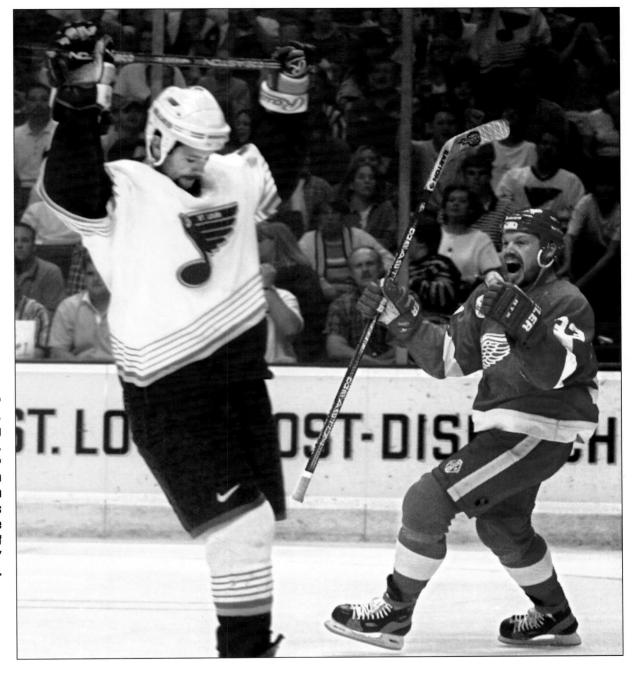

Kris Draper was pumped up, and Craig Conroy wasn't, after Draper assisted on Darren McCarty's goal in the first period of the Wings' 6-1 victory.

ROUND TWO
GAME SIX

Tuesday, May 19, 1998 — The Blues got what they wanted — a return trip to St. Louis — and a lot more than they bargained for.

By Mitch Albom

We now return you to your regularly scheduled Stanley Cup madness.

After a brief interruption in Game 5 — in which aliens from a slow-footed planet occupied the bodies of the Red Wings — the boys were back in form for Game 6, taking care of business in a most businesslike manner. First, they took the measure of their opponents. Then, they ripped their hearts out.

Or, to paraphrase Billie Holliday, I woke up this morning, didn't have no Blues.

The Wings defeated St. Louis, a team many thought would be their toughest opponent, in six games. Why it took six and not five will be a question for the ages, especially when you consider the

Brownie points

Like any good soldier, Doug Brown wanted back in the battle.

His separated left shoulder had healed, only to leave him a casualty of the Red Wings' deep talent pool.

Brown's name didn't disappear from the healthy-scratch list until after the Wings played their most lackluster game of the playoffs in Game 5 against St. Louis.

He wasted no time returning to form. It took Brown less than 15 minutes to help correct the Wings' power-play problems.

Half of Detroit's goals in the 6-1, series-clinching victory against St. Louis came on the power play.

Brown scored at 14:29 of the first period when he came down the left wing, sped over to the face-off circle, and fired a shot that beat Grant Fuhr stick-side for a 2-0 Detroit lead.

It was his first shot of the playoffs.

"It was good to get back," Brown said. "There was a lot of anxiety — you want the body to be well, you don't want to get back too quick. It worked out well."

Brown was injured in the last game of the regular season, April 18 at Colorado. He missed the first 11 games of the playoffs but had been ready to play since about two games into the second-round series. But whereas a guy who scores 19 goals and 42 points and plays the point on power plays would be an automatic re-insertion on almost any other team, it's not that simple in Detroit.

Brown is a perfect fit on the right side of Sergei Fedorov and Slava Kozlov, but in his absence, Wings coach Scotty Bowman had put rugged Tomas Holmstrom on that line.

Holmstrom provided the two Russian playmakers with a solid physical presence, forechecking and going into corners to dig out pucks, leaving Kozlov and Fedorov free to dazzle opponents with their passing.

The line did a bang-up job against the Coyotes in the first round and was the top scoring line against the Blues.

Holmstrom was switched to a line with Steve Yzerman and Darren McCarty, replacing the scratched Brent Gilchrist.

"We had a healthier body that could help us in the back end of the power play ... and it was nice to have a chance to put Brown in," associate coach Barry Smith said.

And the power play, 3-for-35 in the first five games of the series, clicked for three goals with Brown back on the second unit.

As Brown said, it worked out well.

By Helene St. James

---

deftness with which Detroit dispatched the supposedly recharged Blues, 6-1.

"It's a relief to win tonight after the way we blew it on Sunday," said forward Darren McCarty, who opened the scoring for the Wings. "You have to be pumped for 60 minutes. We weren't on Sunday, but we were tonight."

Yes. You could say that. The Wings' first five goals were scored by players better known for grinding than glory. McCarty — who always seems to do things like this when they are most needed — took Kris Draper's winning face-off in the first period and delivered it past Grant Fuhr. That silenced the crowd and slowed the Blues.

Less than three minutes later, Doug Brown, who hadn't played in a month, came down the ice, aimed and fired the puck into the far upper corner of the goal. Considering that was Brown's first shot in 31 days, you gotta admire the accuracy.

"How do you do that when you've been sitting for the past month?" Brown was asked.

He laughed. "A lot of positive mental imagery," he said.

Hmm. Just like Peter Pan. Think good things and you can fly. In which case, Martin Lapointe must have been Tinkerbell. Lapointe — who's quietly becoming a star player — scored Detroit's third and fourth goals, and Tomas Holmstrom got the fifth.

By the third period, the Wings were mostly interested in avoiding injury, and the Blues were thinking about what clubs to put in the bag.

"How do you win like this, in their building, after losing a game like Sunday at home?" center Steve Yzerman was asked.

"Experience," said Yzerman, who had a goal and three assists. "We're the kind of team, if we don't play well one game, we just rebound in the next."

Whenever the Wings hit a bump in the road, they need only look over at Yzerman, who has a quiet way of shrugging off victory and defeat. He might not make a lot of speeches, but in the show-me world of hockey, his attitude, to his teammates, is as good as the Sermon on the Mount.

"We're just playing," he said, with typical head-down humility. "We're all just playing."

And St. Louis isn't anymore. In fact, by the end of the game, most of the Blues fans were on their way home, asking how many home runs Mark McGwire had hit. Meanwhile, inside the Kiel Center, it was hard to tell which was louder, the Detroit fans yelling "We want Dallas!" or the licking chops of Sergei Fedorov's accountants. The Wings star earned his $12-million bonus due when the Wings made the conference finals.

"Has anyone asked you for a loan yet?" Sergei was asked.

"No," he said, looking around the room, "but they haven't showered yet."

Also deserving of a nod was Chris Osgood, who shut down the Blues until Jim Campbell's goal with 5:25 left. Although Osgood has been the object of occasional tongue-clucking doubt, when he needed a big game, he delivered one.

With each series he was growing in stature. More important, he was growing in his own mind toward the star player he deep down feels he is.

"I'm a good goalie, I believe that," Osgood said. "But to be great, to be up there with the Patrick Roys, I have to win. That's the only thing that will do it. I have to win."

Two down.

And now onto the Dallas Stars, another tough team, another team feeling its time has come.

Round Three

Star destroyers

Dallas forward Mike Modano said one reason the Wings were tough was that their forwards — including Darren McCarty, above, shooting against Ed Belfour — got up the ice and into the offensive zone quickly.

Sunday, May 24, 1998 — For the first time in the playoffs, the Red Wings had to open on the road. But that didn't change their game plan.

By Drew Sharp

They're still waiting for the smoke to clear here. Dallas has been in a perpetual haze for a week. The rolling pollution from severe brushfires in Mexico wafted northward, making the sky look as gray and dingy as the mush masquerading as ice at Reunion Arena.

But the city wasn't the only thing looking for fresh air. Its hockey team was in a fog after opening the Western Conference finals with a 2-0 loss to the Red Wings.

The Stars blamed the showing — they managed only 14 shots — on rust from their nine-day layoff.

"Everybody else may be down on us,"

forward Pat Verbeek said, "but nobody's panicking here. We haven't gotten as far as we have by letting one bad game affect us. Everyone needs to realize it was just one game.

"You'll see the real Dallas Stars (in Game 2)."

But everyone here should worry that we probably saw the real Stars in Game 1.

With top scorer Joe Nieuwendyk out after knee surgery, Mike Modano's line was the Stars' only real scoring threat;

Anders
Eriksson
played
keep-away as
Dallas' Mike
Keane played
catch-up
during the
Wings' 2-0
victory, which
the Stars
blamed on a
nine-day
layoff.

It was a little difficult for Matthew Gilchrist when his dad became a Red Wing last summer.

Matthew, 4, had never known his father to play for any team other than Dallas. And he adored Stars center Mike Modano only slightly less than his dad.

But he's right at home in Hockeytown now.

"He feels like a Red Wing now," Brent Gilchrist said. "He's adjusted well. He was a huge Stars fan, but now he's a huge Wings fan.

"He likes Steve Yzerman and Chris Osgood a lot."

The elder Gilchrist made the adjustment pretty well, too, but he admitted being excited about facing the Stars in the Western Conference finals.

"There's no question each game is going to be special," Gilchrist said before Game 1 in Dallas. "It's one thing to play against a former team, but it hasn't been very long since I've played with this club, and it's special.

"Each game here is going to bring a little bit of extra emotion."

Gilchrist, 31, joined the Minnesota North Stars late in the 1992-93 season and moved with them to Dallas, where he played four full seasons.

Did the former Star give any fiery speeches before the game?

"Yeah, I'll tell you, there wasn't a dry eye in the room," Larry Murphy said between chuckles. "No, no speeches, but he was obviously excited about the game, and what a position to be in, playing your ex-teammates in the conference finals.

"He was really glad when the game got under way. I think the waiting wasn't easy for him."

Gilchrist, who missed the final six weeks of the regular season because of a groin injury, played in five of the six games against Dallas and scored a goal in Game 3 before reinjuring his groin.

By Helene St. James

the other lines were basically grinders and checkers. Modano fired two shots at Chris Osgood, and his wingers had none.

Even after one game, it was apparent the Wings were frustrating Modano just as they had Phoenix's Jeremy Roenick and St. Louis' Brett Hull.

"I felt bad for Mike, to be honest with you," Stars defenseman Derian Hatcher said. "He had guys hanging all over his back."

Modano said: "You know, we've won in the past when I haven't scored. We had a great series last series when I didn't score. It'd be nice to get some now, but it'd be nice to have everybody score."

That's the way the Wings win, with all four lines grinding away and goals likely to come from any of them. On this day, Slava Kozlov and Martin Lapointe provided the scoring in the second period.

"Lapointe, Darren McCarty and those guys get up the ice very well," Modano said. "That's what makes them dangerous — they can hit, they can get rebounds and play good defense, and go on offense and make great plays. And they've all got great shots.

"When you have those type of

players chipping in goals, it's tough to beat them."

It was the first taste of what the Stars' big defense and generally older and smaller forwards would have to contend with — the Wings' size, speed and depth up front.

"Our goal is to battle," Brendan Shanahan said. "I think we wore down St. Louis, regardless of the four-game sweep and the long break that they had before they played us.

"No one guy can do it by himself. We have to stick with what we're doing, and that's roll them over as a team, and four lines and everybody chipping away, because Dallas has some monsters back there. We all have a responsibility to drive the net and make people work."

The Wings weren't ready to take the Stars for granted, but you couldn't help but sense a quiet confidence in the Wings that wasn't there following the starts of the previous two series.

"We've yet to be 2-0 in the playoffs so far," Kris Draper said, "so that's definitely a motivational factor for us. We're not satisfied with just getting a split here.

"We're in a great position to try and take control of this series, and we don't want to miss the opportunity."

Shooting Stars hit back

Tuesday, May 26, 1998 — After losing Game 1 at home, the Stars were desperate to show their fans — and the Red Wings — what they were made of.

By Mitch Albom

Brendan Shanahan, center, did his best to shake up Stars goalie Ed Belfour, but Belfour wouldn't rattle in Dallas' victory, which evened the series.

First, he shoved the Stars' best player, Mike Modano, and knocked him to the ice like a bully flooring a schoolkid. Then he flipped another Dallas star, Pat Verbeek, stripping his helmet as he was sent sprawling.

The ref blew the whistle and pointed — you, mister, I mean you — and the Detroit Bad Boy snarled and shook his head.

And this is our goalie.

It was that kind of night in the Lone Star State. We had goalies playing sumo wrestlers and tough guys taking fists to the face without retaliation. We had shooters missing shots and non-scorers scoring goals.

We had a game that proved you can't sum up a series based on the first game.

"That's a pretty good hockey team over there," Darren McCarty said after the Stars won, 3-1, and evened the Western Conference finals at one victory apiece. "It was a physical game, for sure. But you do what you have to do to win. Sometimes, there are liberties taken."

Liberties? If the elbows, fists and sticks that flew were liberties, then "give me liberty or give me death" might be a toss-up.

Then again, it was that type of game. Experts thought they had this series wrapped up after the Red Wings' opening victory, when Detroit played good defense, just enough offense and won convincingly.

But this was a different night. Different in attitude, different in result. Here was Dallas, being told its offense would come from Modano or nobody. But here were grinders Bob Bassen and Greg Adams putting the puck past Chris Osgood, and Guy Carbonneau scoring an empty-net goal.

What happened was this: Dallas got desperate. And physical. Very physical. In previous games, when opposing teams were foolish enough to go to the penalty box, the Wings eventually made them pay.

Not in Game 2. Detroit's on-again, off-again power play was off again and went 0-for-6.

"In a close series like this, a power-play goal can make the difference," Steve Yzerman said. "We have to find a way to make it work."

And find more ways to beat Ed Belfour, who made 27 saves and allowed only Slava Kozlov's second-period goal.

"We just couldn't get anything by Belfour," McCarty said. "He's going to make the first save, and then they clear it before we can get any chance for a rebound. And as you saw, he's not afraid to mix it up."

That is why the Stars outbid other potential suitors for Eddie the Eagle when he became a free agent during the

off-season. They needed someone in net tough enough and, yes, even crazy enough to keep the Red Wings from pushing him around, should they meet in the championship stage.

Belfour didn't back down.

"There was never any panic on this team after the first game," said Belfour, who recorded his sixth career victory in 27 games against the Wings. "It was just one game. We got back to the style of play that we like. We got a little more physical at both ends of the ice."

Belfour, momentarily forgetting the wisdom of avoiding those who are four inches taller and 40 pounds heavier, traded swipes with Brendan Shanahan during a Wings power play in the second period.

"They wanted to bang me in front of the net," Belfour said, "so I just banged right back. I don't know if (Shanahan) was getting frustrated. I don't think about that stuff. It's just part of the game."

It lifted the Stars and the crowd, which erupted approvingly with a high-decibel chant, "Ed-die! Ed-die!"

Soon thereafter, Osgood delivered a shot to Verbeek, who was flying toward him. It didn't matter that it was a Kris Draper shove that propelled Verbeek. Osgood made a statement.

After a pulseless opener that exhibited all the life of an Al Gore

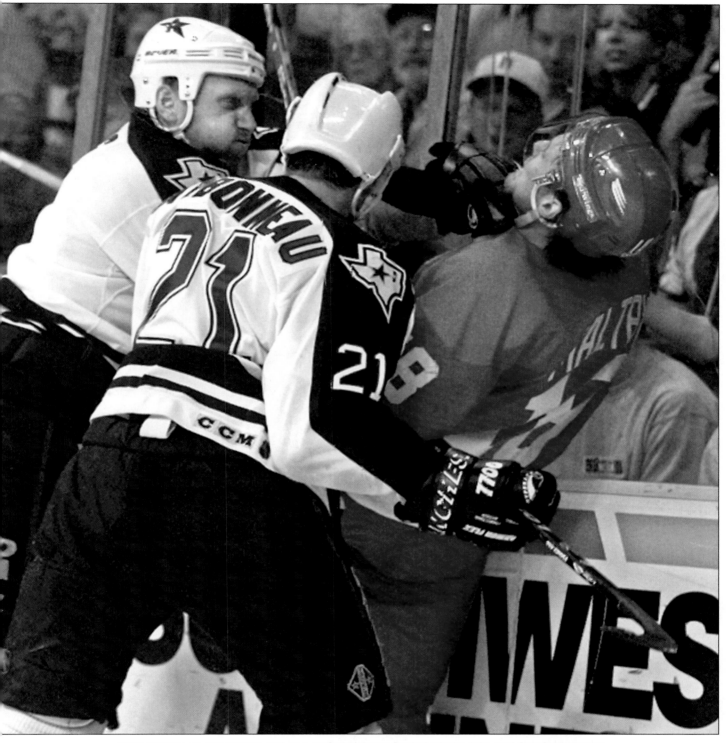

Kirk Maltby, on the wrong end of a greeting from Craig Ludwig, left, and Guy Carbonneau, proved that sometimes keeping your chin up is sometimes a bad thing.

speech, Game 2 injected some much-needed passion and a bit of residual hatred into the series.

"We knew they would come out fighting because we all knew how important this game was for them,"

Wings defenseman Larry Murphy said. "They had a little more fire in them, and we tried to match it as much as we could.

"Once they got a lead, you knew that they were going to sit back and get into their tight defensive system."

Now it was the Wings' turn to respond to a loss.

"I look at the positive," McCarty said. "We came down here and got one."

And the Stars looked at their positive; they were headed north tied.

Ticket muster

One look at Fairview Avenue in Sterling Heights before the Red Wings played Dallas and most Detroiters might have said, "Well, there goes the neighborhood."

The parents of Stars defenseman Shawn Chambers, left, who grew up five houses from teammate Derian Hatcher, painted a Dallas logo on their lawn.

They took the logo out of a game program, scaled it up on a computer, then spent an entire day making their neighbors see red.

"I did this in 1995," when Shawn played for New Jersey, John Chambers said. "Nobody came and trashed it then, so I thought I'd do it again."

Other Stars were scrambling for extra tickets to games at Joe Louis Arena for family and friends, too: Mike Modano grew up in Highland, Dan Keczmer is from Mt. Clemens, and Jason Botterill played at Michigan.

The NHL allots 50 seats per game for each team, and that leaves only four or five per player.

As Keczmer said, "Something's got to give. I think we could all use 20 or 30."

Got any extra tickets?

"It's a madhouse," Botterill said. "No one wants to be the one left short."

While he confessed to not being a Wings fan — the team wasn't exactly in its glory years when he was growing up — even Modano liked the idea of playing in Hockeytown.

"The novelty of playing Detroit has kind of worn off, but this makes it special again in a way," Modano said. "It's a great opportunity to make a statement against the defending champions in your own backyard.

"I have everything but a championship. A win in this series, to get to the finals. . . . I could turn the corner and get my career going. To do it in Detroit, that would be even better."

By Nicholas J. Cotsonika

Martin Lapointe celebrated his third-period goal that put a lid on a Dallas comeback — and the game out of reach, 5-3.

Yes! No! Uh-oh. Yes!

Friday, May 29, 1998 — The Red Wings came home intent on delivering an early knockout blow. They almost lulled themselves to sleep in the process.

By Mitch Albom

So which part do you want to hear about? The Dream, the Sleep, the Nightmare or the Wake-Up? You can say a lot about the Red Wings; you can't say they didn't give you a taste of everything in Game 3.

The first chunk of evening was too good to be true, shots deflecting off opponents' skates into the net, the scoreboard flipping like a pinball machine. One goal. Two goals. Three. Four. A dream, right?

The next chunk was a deep sleep, the Wings snoring through a couple of Dallas goals, sagging, rolling over, enjoying the pillow of their lead.

The third chunk was a nightmare, when, less than halfway through the third period, Mike Modano shoved a puck under Chris Osgood's legs, and suddenly it was a one-goal lead, and the Wings were wiping their eyes like firefighters caught in their pajamas.

The final chunk was putting the fire out in the frantic closing minutes. Wake up. The house is burning.

Finally, when Martin Lapointe swooped behind the Stars' net, left goalie Ed Belfour sprawling on the ice, and curled back in front for a quick shot through the pads of the desperately returning Belfour — well, the night had its ending, and the fans had their money's worth.

And coach Scotty Bowman had a few of his remaining hairs turn gray.

"We got caught watching the scoreboard," Bowman said after the Wings blew three-quarters of a 4-0 lead before bouncing back for a 5-3 victory at Joe Louis Arena and a 2-1 advantage in the Western Conference finals.

"We were just dumping the puck in the neutral zone," Bowman said. "Things were almost going too well for us early."

It took Belfour's attempt to draw a penalty and scramble to get back in the net to kill the Stars' rally.

"How hard did you hit Belfour?" Lapointe was asked after the victory.

"Shheeesh," he said, rolling his eyes.

"Well, did you hit him at all?"

"I hit his stick," he said. "He went for a dive. That's when I knew to go right in front of the net and shoot."

The Wings had their quiet men to thank for their victory.

One goal came from Jamie Macoun, maybe the most under-interviewed player on the Wings; another from Brent Gilchrist, the second-most under-interviewed player; and two came from Nick Lidstrom, who often speaks to open notebooks but very rarely fills a page.

A few more words on Lidstrom.

Here he was on a power play, and he sent a screamer to the net that dinged off Derian Hatcher's skate, smacked into Belfour's inner leg, and ricocheted into the net for a 2-0 lead. Minnesota Fats

Brendan Shanahan gives Nick Lidstrom, left, a hearty pat after one of Lidstrom's two goals. Both of Lidstrom's goals bounced off players on their way into the net. "I got lucky tonight," he said.

couldn't have made that shot.

Here was Lidstrom again, whizzing another shot that smoked past Belfour's left shoulder for a 3-0 lead.

"I got lucky tonight," Lidstrom said. "We talked about putting shots on net and hoping for rebounds and bounces. Both of my goals hit other guys on the way in."

Of course, Lidstrom's night would have been washed away if the Wings hadn't been able to hold the lead.

"When you have a 4-0 lead, you don't have a lot of adrenaline," Lapointe admitted. "We had to find it, fast."

And even though they did, Dallas made as much of a point in this game as Detroit.

The Stars could have folded like pita bread, given up the chase and saved it for another night. There are few things as uphill as a four-goal deficit in another team's building — especially when the other team is the defending Stanley Cup champion — but the Stars played as if programmed by a computer.

They kept coming, even as some

Wings fans were leaving. They seemed unaffected by their deficit, chasing loose pucks, stealing passes, breaking up chances. They were rewarded with two goals by Jere Lehtinen, then Modano's to make it 4-3 with 12:26 left.

"They probably feel they should have won this game," Macoun said later. "And who knows? Maybe they should have."

Let Detroit take that as a warning.

For now, there was the victory, the Sunrise after the Dream, the Sleep, the Nightmare and the Wake-Up.

There also was this: Home was sweet. That was a change. At least half the time in this playoff march, the Joe had been less a friend than a foe. Familiarity bred contentment. Contentment meant a loss.

This night, there was only enough contentment for a scare. When the final horn sounded, the Wings exhaled, and the PA system played "Oh, What a Night."

You could say that again. Wake us for Game 4.

This day's big win wasn't on the ice

Kirk Maltby was rarin' to go while celebrating his first-period goal.

Sunday, May 31, 1998 — There isn't much that could overshadow a hockey game at Joe Louis Arena, much less one in the conference finals. But there was on this day.

By Helene St. James

The tune had not been played at Joe Louis Arena for almost a year. "Bad to the Bone" is Vladdie's song, and it didn't seem right to play it without him around.

But about 25 minutes after Game 4's opening face-off, there were the familiar guitar licks. Da da da da dum.

It could mean only one thing.

The fans looked around, and the Red Wings looked up. The game wasn't so important just then.

An old friend had come home. His face filled the scoreboard.

Fans turned to owner Mike Ilitch's luxury box high over the Zamboni gate and jumped to their feet when they caught sight of Vladimir Konstantinov waving with his left hand. Sergei Mnatsakanov sat by his side.

Cheers of "Vlad-die! Vlad-die! Vlad-die!" reverberated for a good two minutes. On the ice, Wings and Stars

alike tapped their sticks in welcome, greeting one of hockey's all-time best players.

"I saw him when everybody stand up, and I'm almost crying," forward Slava Kozlov said. "I appreciate that people still love Vladdie and remember Vladdie and Sergei. It's a great feeling to see them here. I have incredible feeling right now."

Fittingly, Kozlov scored the goal with 8:30 left in regulation that gave the Wings a 3-2 victory — and a commanding 3-1 lead in the Western Conference finals.

Although the moment was brief, seeing Konstantinov in the box tore at Nick Lidstrom's heart, too.

There was his buddy, his fearsome defensive partner with whom he had shared the greatest moment possible in hockey, winning the Stanley Cup.

"I got chills when they were introduced and everybody was standing up cheering," Lidstrom said.

"It was a great moment," Steve Yzerman said. "For a moment, you can think about how special those guys were and are to our team."

But no one had to wrestle back his feelings any harder than defenseman Slava

Vladimir Konstantinov, center, his wife, Irina, and Sergei Mnatsakanov caught the excitement of the Joe Louis Arena crowd, which erupted when the presence of the former defenseman and team masseur was announced.

Fetisov. He was in the limousine accident with Konstantinov and Mnatsakanov June 13, 1997, and has lived with the unanswerable question: Why not me?

"If not for an inch," Fetisov said later, his voice a near whisper, "maybe it is me up there in that box, and not on the ice. . . .

"I wake up in the night sometimes, I see the pictures in my head, but I cannot find an answer. Why this happen to Vladimir and Sergei and did not happen to me, too?"

Fetisov also was injured in the accident, but he was released from the hospital while Konstantinov and Mnatsakanov remained in comas.

The two men, Fetisov and Konstantinov, were more than teammates; they were like brothers.

Fetisov's real younger brother — who, back in Russia, had been best buddies with Konstantinov — died in a car crash when he was 17.

As fans and players gave him a warm welcome home, Konstantinov smiled and held onto a white pom-pom with his left hand and swung it back and forth, then waved. Mnatsakanov, the former team masseur, raised his right arm and

Meanwhile, on the ice and on the bench, the Wings held back tears and paid tribute by tapping their sticks on the ice and against the boards.

Yee-OUCH!

By Steve Schrader

Grown men cringed when they saw the replay.

When a slash to Martin Lapointe's leg didn't deliver its intended message, Dallas goalie Ed Belfour — once again showing why some call him "Psycho" — whipped his stick up between Lapointe's legs.

Ouch!

Lapointe went down in pain but skated to the bench screaming at the goalie all the way.

" 'Just keep coming!' " he yelled at Belfour.

Referee Dan Marouelli penalized Belfour for tripping (perhaps he was referring to Belfour's mental state). With the Red Wings already on the power play, that gave them 39 seconds of 5-on-3.

Lapointe said he was more than willing to take, uh, one for the team.

"I'll take that all night for us to go on the power play," Lapointe said. "I was just hoping we'd score a power-play goal."

Stars center Bob Bassen, serving the original penalty, was out of the box but still far from the play when captain Steve Yzerman's power-play goal gave the Wings a 2-0 first-period lead.

Perhaps Belfour was upset at surrendering a shorthanded goal to Kirk Maltby about four minutes earlier. Or maybe he remembered Lapointe scored the insurance goal in the Wings' Game 3 victory.

"Yeah," Lapointe said. "He probably lost his cool."

The Stars overcame Belfour's lapse of control and tied the game at 2 with a second-period goal by Pat Verbeek and a power-play score by Sergei Zubov 55 seconds into the third.

Slava Kozlov scored the winner with 8:30 left in the Wings' 3-2 victory in Game 4.

Lapointe said the shot from Belfour smarted, but it wasn't quite as bad as it looked.

"He didn't get the right spot," Lapointe said, "but he got pretty close. You take your chances when you get near the crease, but I don't like that kind of stuff.

Martin Lapointe collapsed — who wouldn't? — after this vicious groin slash from Ed Belfour.

"I'm just glad that we made (Belfour) pay for taking that shot at me."

Certainly no male fan would blame him, but Lapointe was chagrined at falling.

"He just speared me there, and I've got a mark to prove it," he said. "He tried to put it right in my groin area. I went down because he hurt me. I got right back up, but I don't like to go down. I don't go down much."

Did the hit deserve a suspension?

"I don't know, but it should have at least been a five-minute penalty," Lapointe said. "It's a good thing he didn't get me in the right spot."

The league decided two minutes was enough, even though Lapointe could have been severely injured.

"He's a young guy, and he's married, too," coach Scotty Bowman said. "It's totally uncalled for."

Postscript: After the Wings clinched the series and another trip to the Stanley Cup finals, Lapointe was asked, "Was it worth that shot to your groin?"

"Oh, yeah, it was worth it," he said. "I'd even take another one."

rustled his pom-pom, energetically pumping his fist.

"It was emotional," Igor Larionov said. "I guess everybody was kind of, how do you say, everything was coming back from last summer."

Konstantinov, 31, relayed through his wife, Irina, that he was nervous and excited about attending the game. But like the warrior he is, no nerves showed. Just smiles.

When Kirk Maltby scored the Wings' first goal, Konstantinov took his pom-pom and waved. Mnatsakanov broke out in a smile and lifted his right arm toward his wife, Ylena, who reached out her left hand to him. Together, the Mnatsakanovs clapped hands and cheered every Wings goal, the longest after Kozlov scored the winner.

The game capped an emotional three days for Konstantinov, who returned to Detroit after spending winter and spring rehabilitating in South Florida. The day before Game 4, he joined his teammates for practice, and saw his locker, decorated with mementos and all his old stuff.

"He's still with us even when he's not," forward Doug Brown said. "His locker is always ready for him anytime he wants to show up. It was really special today and yesterday at practice. He was cheerful and smiling. When you see him happy, it touches everybody."

Konstantinov greeted his teammates by name and shook hands with some.

"He's not a different person than what he was the day before the injury," Irina Konstantinov said. "He's absolutely himself. The doctors explained that the injury can change a person's habits and their nature. But Vladdie is himself."

Konstantinov still struggled with short-term memory — he could not remember having been to the White House on Jan. 30 and likely wouldn't remember Game 4 for long.

"A few days after this, he probably won't remember that we were here," Irina Konstantinov said. "He does remember the Stanley Cup, but not all the celebration, which is very sad, because I would rather see him remember every moment of it. It was such a wonderful time."

The wonderful time lasted six days. Almost a year later, Konstantinov amazed doctors with his physical recovery. He was able to hold his head up by himself and use his left hand and arm, and walk a little with assistance. Verbal skills were coming along a bit slower.

"For some reason he refuses to talk in English," Fetisov said. "He speaks in Russian. He's improved a lot since I see him last time. He looks much better since the Olympic break."

The Konstantinovs left about halfway through the third period. After the game, Mnatsakanov paid a short visit to his friends in the locker room.

"He saw my goal, and Sergei told me 'great job,' and he was very happy," Kozlov said. "And I'm happy, too."

They're game

By Mitch Albom

Look, I'm not trying to make excuses for these guys. But hockey is a rough business. The Red Wings need a release. They need to blow off steam. So, OK, maybe it isn't "normal" behavior. But they're big, powerful men. They have to do it. They gotta have it.

They need their chess.

Chess? "We're into it," admits Darren McCarty.

Chess? "Oh, yeah, every chance we get," says Brendan Shanahan.

Chess? Chess. On the team plane. In the hotels. In the locker room. It might be Bobby Orr on the ice, but it's Bobby Fischer everywhere else.

"Last year it was card games, poker, helicopter, stuff like that," McCarty says. "And for a while this year it was Balderdash and Scattergories."

"And suddenly chess became popular?" I say.

He shrugs. "Brendan brought in a board."

Brendan brought in a board? That's it? And that's how the defending Stanley Cup champions spend their spare time, deciding whether the knight should take the rook?

"Sometimes we play two on a side," McCarty says. "It's like a war. Other guys line up behind you, trying to figure out the best move."

Let's face it. Only hockey gives you this. A bunch of guys with scars and missing teeth gathered around a chess board is either the greatest endorsement ever for the NHL or a sure sign the players have taken too many blows to the head.

"Who's the best player on the team?" I ask Shanahan.

"Iggy," he says.

"Who's the best player on the team?" I ask McCarty.

"Iggy."

Let's go to Iggy.

Igor Larionov has always been more cerebral than your average player. He grew up in Russia, a nation quite fond of chess, and began playing the game when he was 6.

"Have you ever lost?" I ask.

"One time," Larionov says.

"Impressive," I say.

He winces. We look around at his teammates, pulling on jockstraps and throwing towels.

"Consider the competition?" I say.

"Exactly," he sighs.

So, OK. It might not be Moscow. Maybe some of the Wings still think Boris Spassky is Natasha's sidekick on "Rocky & Bullwinkle." But you gotta admit, chess is a preferred pastime to smoking dope, chasing women or making the police blotter — all of which seem to be fairly popular in other sports.

Chess uses your brain. It passes the time. And as one Wing says, "It's really hard to lose money on it."

But knowing the Wings, they probably throw themselves headfirst into chess. You just hope no fights break out over who plays black and who plays white.

"Mathieu Dandenault's surprisingly good," McCarty says. "Sometimes he teams with Martin Lapointe."

"Yeah," adds Joey Kocur, "but then they start speaking French, and nobody knows if they're cheating. That's not fair."

We should point out that playing games has a long tradition on this Detroit team. They're popular for a while, but then fade out.

"Somebody throws a game out there and suddenly we're all into it," McCarty says, "but we do it so much, we get sick of it, and then we never want to see it again."

McCarty says Trivial Pursuit is beginning to grow in popularity. It could be the Next Official Pastime of the Best Team in the NHL.

"We were playing the other day, and the winning question was, 'What hockey coach led Montreal, Pittsburgh and Detroit to the Stanley Cup?'" McCarty says.

"That's convenient," I say.

"Yeah, but Shanahan said he was going to tell Scotty that I didn't know the answer."

Boys will be boys.

Which is the whole point. Boys will be boys. So I am not going to bury this story about chess. I am printing it for the whole world to see because we in Detroit are not embarrassed that our team has brains and brawn. We are not ashamed that they like little plastic kings and queens.

We are proud. We are glad.

Wings lose that lucky feeling

Wednesday, June 3, 1998 — The Stars complained their 3-1 series deficit was a result of the Red Wings' catching all the breaks, all the lucky bounces. But just when the Wings were on the verge of closing them out, the luck made a shocking shift.

By Mitch Albom

They were 85 seconds away from the big room, the bright lights, the top floor of the highest skyscraper, the Stanley Cup finals — and then a Big Dallas Taxi splashed dirty water all over their skates.

Coming home. There will be a Game 6 in these Western Conference finals, because the Stars never gave up and because Detroit could not ride Lady Luck forever.

More than a few times, the Red Wings had been saved by the brilliant play of goalie Chris Osgood, the fortunate flick of a defenseman's stick or the misfire of a Dallas shot. Not all of this is luck, but some of it is. No big deal. All teams need a little. Most get some eventually.

But the Stars were just about convinced that they had forgotten to send in their destiny dues.

That is, until Guy Carbonneau — who I believe is 102 years old — fired a youthfully hopeful shot from the right of the Wings' net with 85 seconds left in the third period — and in the Dallas season. It was not what you'd call a high-percentage shot.

But it hit Nick Lidstrom's stick and clanged over Osgood, tying the score at 2.

So much for a quick flight home.

The Dallas fans were re-energized. Reunion Arena began to thump. And Lady Luck had found a new boyfriend.

Forty-six seconds into overtime, Jamie Langenbrunner, who had not scored a goal in the playoffs, fired a skipping shot from center ice that Osgood would stop 99 out of 100 times. This was time No. 100.

Stars win, 3-2.

"They tied it up, they took a shot, and they won it," said a shrugging Steve

Scotty Bowman exhaled — too soon — as the teams prepared for overtime after Dallas tied the game with 85 seconds remaining.

Yzerman, putting a captain-like spin on the defeat.

"Are you worried about bouncing back for Game 6?" someone asked.

"I don't see it as bouncing back," he said. "I see it as moving on."

Wise. Very wise.

Eighty-five bleeping seconds!

Even though the Wings were clinging to a one-goal lead for what seemed like eternity, it had felt like a night of Detroit destiny. The Stars were everywhere in the first period, blocking shots, stealing passes, putting the puck into Osgood's pads, chest, shoulder. They finally took the lead on Mike Keane's goal at 14:16.

But with less than a minute to play in the period, Craig Ludwig yanked Martin Lapointe to the ice by his neck. A whistle blew. A power play was on. Moments later, Larry Murphy's wobbly shot was re-directed by Tomas Holmstrom, trickled over Ed Belfour, and the game was tied at 1.

A tie? This, despite the Stars' more than doubling the Wings' shots in the

period and more than doubling their hustle? A tie?

Yep. That kind of night. In the second period, Igor Larionov got crashed against the boards, got up dizzy, missed his chance to go to the bench, and started down the ice instead. Next thing he knew, Lidstrom was firing him a pass, and, with little else to do, Larionov fired a long shot.

It went past Belfour for a 2-1 Wings lead at 3:40 of the period. It was the Wings' seventh shot.

But that's why they play 60 minutes, not 58. The Stars deserved to win. They won more face-offs. They had more shots. They never gave up.

"People were criticizing us for saying it," Mike Modano said, "but we believed we outplayed them in Detroit. And we knew coming into this game that if we kept playing the same way, it was just going to be a matter of time before things started going our way."

Now, remember that the buildup to this game was filled with accusations by the Stars, who seemed to feel that fate was treating them like a dog who just soiled the carpet.

"They know the deal," Benoit Hogue sniped at the Wings. "They know they've been floating on their luck."

Until those late goals, Osgood was the story of this game. His hot play kept the Wings alive all night.

How would he rebound from the shocking end and the scrutiny that would follow?

"Don't underestimate Ozzie's toughness," Yzerman warned. "I'm not worried about him at all."

"We lose as a team," added coach Scotty Bowman, reverting to the proper defense for his goalie.

That was the plan: Forget about the 85 seconds, forget about Langenbrunner's shot. Act as if it were the most normal of losses, no big deal, inevitable against a good team that could not be held down forever.

And then just hope that Dallas doesn't spend the next day inhaling the fumes of its miracle. You don't want to mess with a destiny like that.

Chris Osgood started his retreat from the ice before the puck came to rest after Jamie Langenbrunner's 90-foot blast won the game for the Stars with less than a minute gone in overtime.

Chris Osgood, above, used everything he had, including the butt end of his stick, to shut out the Stars for the second time in the series. Ed Belfour, right, started the game in a hole after Larry Murphy put Darren McCarty's feed past the Dallas keeper.

Osgood silences the critics

Friday, June 5, 1998 — The question everyone asked as the series returned to Detroit was, "What is Chris Osgood made of?" They liked the answer.

By Mitch Albom

After the game, Ed Belfour paid his respects to Chris Osgood with a handshake. Many fans showed their respect before the game, by giving the goalie loud chants of "Oz-zie! Oz-zie!" when the starting lineups were introduced.

In the end, you could no more stop them than you could stop the moon. They rose to the occasion, they rose to the challenge, and finally — when the last seconds ticked away and Chris Osgood threw his hands into the air and leaped into a hug from Larry Murphy as a lonesome octopus came flying onto the ice — finally, they raised the roof.

The Red Wings were back to the big stage, the Stanley Cup finals, and they burst through the curtain with a certain swagger, as if they knew it would happen, as if they'd been there before.

Of course they had, and that was the difference. If you want to know why the Wings came out Friday as if storming the last bridge out of hell and banged and slammed and dug and dazzled and never stopped until the horn sounded — well, here it is. They knew what they wanted. They knew what it takes. They knew how to do it.

Turn out the Stars, their party's over. The Wings delivered a game so thorough, so dynamic, that if you painted it you'd need fluorescent colors; if you wrote it, you'd need two boxes of paper. They ended the series the way they began it, with a 2-0 shutout. And more important, with a message that said, "Hey, folks, we're the defending champs, remember? You still have to get through us."

"What did you say to Ozzie when you hugged him?" Murphy was asked after the Wings won their third conference title in four years.

"I didn't say anything," Murphy answered, smiling. "And neither did he. It was a moment, that's all."

He laughed. "We had a moment."

Didn't we all? For all the endless drama of the playoffs, only one favorite was still standing as they headed into the finals, and it was Detroit. There were no 90-foot goals. No bad ricochets. And no Dallas Stars complaining that they weren't getting any "luck."

"We rebound well," said captain Steve Yzerman, who, in politely accepting the Clarence Campbell Bowl, was already in his finals mode of cautious understatement.

Rebound well? Uh. Yeah. If Game 5 was the series' low point, then Game 6 was its high. Just playing in Joe Louis Arena, where outside temperatures were appropriately, for hockey, in the low 50s — not the low 100s as they were in Dallas — seemed to energize the night. The Wings were back to flying, leaving their opponents reading the names on the backs of their jerseys.

And that's when they do their damage. It began — fittingly — when the Wings were down a man in the first period. Darren McCarty beat opponents to an Yzerman pass, came down the ice, and waited until he spotted Murphy, who took the cross-ice feed and put a backhander through Ed Belfour. Score: 1-0. That wounded the Stars. The next goal put them on the critical list. In the second period, Sergei Fedorov took a dump pass from Murphy and shot as he came across the middle. There was no deflection. There was no screen. There was just the puck, Belfour and embarrassment, as the rubber

dribbled through him and left him hiding his head in disbelief.

Now, if we're going to dole out individual kudos, we must begin with the first man onto the ice and the last line of defense: goalie Chris Osgood.

Critics who panned Osgood for missing an overtime gimme in Game 5 must have missed the first 58 minutes of that contest, and surely they were stunned at what they saw in Game 6. Because here was no shrinking violet, no thumb-sucking little kid. Here was a young man growing up before our eyes. Sure, Osgood talked bravely after the embarrassment of Game 5. But only his play would prove the starch in his backbone.

Does anyone want to argue now? Osgood — who recorded two shutouts in the series — was everywhere, blocking them high, low, on his knees, on his stomach.

He took a two-on-none break and stopped Mike Keane's shot while on the ice. He took a Mike Modano whacker from six feet away and blocked it into the air. He stopped a hard shot by Jamie Langenbrunner — who put the winner past him in Game 5 — and said, "Sorry. Your free pass is up."

He went left, right and flat-out for glory. He took all the stones thrown at him and threw them back through the looking glass.

"It used to be people didn't talk about me at all," he said, "and now, I really don't care what they say. That's as plain

Whoop, there's Larry

By Jason La Canfora and
Helene St. James

He will be harassed whenever the puck comes near. He will be scorned and ridiculed by 19,000 fans every time he rushes up ice.

Whooop, whooop, whooop.

The sound will echo throughout the MCI Center in Washington. Red Wings defenseman Larry Murphy will be the target. He can already hear it.

The former Capital couldn't have been happier: He was heading back to Washington, where he's less than revered, for the Stanley Cup finals.

Murphy scored a shorthanded goal and assisted on another in the 2-0 victory over Dallas that clinched the Western Conference finals in six games.

His two shorthanded goals and three shorthanded points through the conference finals were as many as any Wing mustered through the 82-game regular season.

"Larry Murphy was outstanding," said associate coach Dave Lewis, Murphy's first NHL defensive partner. "Besides the goals, he was breaking up plays, doing everything.

"It looked like he had a 40-foot stick. He was everywhere. He just played everything perfectly."

Larry Murphy, left, has found plenty of friends in Detroit, including Darren McCarty.

Detroit was poised to become the first champion to repeat since Pittsburgh in 1992, a club that Wings coach Scotty Bowman coached and Murphy played for. Four more victories and the moniker "Team of the '90s" just might fit.

The term Future Hall of Famer already suited Murphy.

He has shone since joining the Wings at the 1997 trade deadline; they admit they might not have won the Cup last year without him.

"He is such a good player," said Nicklas Lidstrom, Murphy's defense partner.

"He's always open for a pass. He's always there to help you out in the corners.

"That's been a big help to my game — he stays pretty close to me on the ice for an outlet pass or if a guy is coming down one-on-one on me, he's always coming over, staying close.

"Playing with Murph has really helped my game this year."

Murphy is third on the all-time scoring list for defensemen with 1,103 points. He finished fifth among defensemen this season with 52 points and led the Wings with a plus-35 rating.

Yet, Detroit is Murphy's sixth NHL team in 18 seasons. He has been passed around from franchise to franchise, booed out of places such as Toronto.

"Ill winds were blowing," said Jamie Macoun, who was rescued from the Maple Leafs this season. "They picked on Larry because a couple times he got caught on the power play, and he really had no support.

"In essence, he was seeing plays some of the players in Toronto couldn't see, so it wasn't as good a fit. But with the talent here, he's seeing plays, and the others are reading them the same way, so it's really working out well for him."

Murphy left Washington in 1989, but he still is remembered there with that derisive chant.

Whooop, whooop, whooop.

"I hope I hear it again," he said. "We're just so excited about winning the series, we'll worry about the next one tomorrow."

as I can say it. I know, and my teammates know, that I've been playing great since the second game of the Phoenix series. Goals will go in. But I'm just trying to get us to win."

Osgood is one of the few Wings who didn't really contribute in last year's miracle run. He has a championship ring, but when he slides it on, it can't feel the way he wants it to feel. He wants one that comes with memories, his memories.

"More than any single player on this team," Brendan Shanahan said, "Ozzie wants to win this thing."

Of course, this was a team thing. Which is what made Game 6 so satisfying. There wasn't one guy in red who didn't come out sweating and come off panting.

Here was McCarty, playing half the night without his helmet, because collisions kept knocking it off. Here was Fedorov, slamming Derian Hatcher into the boards, even though the Stars captain oversizes Sergei by four inches and 25 pounds. Here was Yzerman, digging at everything that moved, and Murphy, playing

Seconds after Steve Yzerman accepted the Clarence Campbell Bowl, he whisked it off the ice. His team had a bigger chalice on its shopping list.

so much younger than his years. Here was Jamie Macoun, decking Modano so hard that Modano lay on the ice as the action continued around him, half in pain, half in disbelief.

As Murphy said, they had a moment. A group motivated by a desire to return to glory, and to persevere against the tragedy that six days after last year's Cup took two of their family away from the fold.

"Were you thinking of Vladimir Konstantinov and Sergei Mnatsakanov tonight?" someone asked Fedorov.

"I think of them all the time at moments like this," he answered. "There is no stronger motivation for me than to celebrate a win this year for longer than six days."

Well said.

That's a stretch

Sergei Fedorov closed in, but couldn't quite get the angle on Washington goalie Olaf Kolzig, and his shot sailed through the crease.

Previous page: The Wings' Joey Kocur got the bum's rush from Kolzig's crease by Calle Johansson in Game 1, but Kocur had his revenge — the first goal of the Stanley Cup finals.

Tuesday, June 9, 1998 — One obstacle remained between the Red Wings and their second straight Stanley Cup: the surprising Washington Capitals, who finished fourth in the Eastern Conference but marched to the finals through Boston, Ottawa and Buffalo.

By Mitch Albom

On a night when they reached for the highest heights, the story would be summed up by a man on his belly.

Here was Darren McCarty, in the third period of this surprisingly tight Stanley Cup finals opener, and he saw trouble coming. Washington's Joe Juneau was coming in unchecked on goalie Chris Osgood.

McCarty was too far behind to block him, too far away to hit him, there simply wasn't enough of McCarty to do what was needed.

So he did the only thing he could: He elongated himself. Went bellyfirst, stick out, stretched from six feet standing to about 10 feet lying down, and got his stick on the puck just before Juneau could get off a shot. The play ended with a whimper, not a bang — and as much could be said of the rest of the night.

Caps Capped. Wings Win. The score was 2-1, in a game that wasn't a showcase for NHL excitement. But what did you expect? Art? A blowout?

Hey. These are the Stanley Cup finals. You win on your knees, you win on your belly, you win on a bed of nails if you have to.

People always focus on goals that are made, but the story of this one was the goals that were not. And better yet, the shots that never were. The Red Wings took a team that averaged 30 shots a game against its previous opponent, and held it to 17.

So it wasn't a shooting gallery. It was two early goals by the Wings and a night of guarding the treasure. It was Osgood

The Capitals' Olaf Kolzig sent this shot into a safe orbit in the third period, but two saves he failed to make in the first period were enough for the Wings.

making tremendous saves, catching hot pucks in his glove, stopping point-blank shots when no one was there to help.

It was 2-0 in the first period. It was 2-1 after two. And finally it was that furious closing segment, when the Wings realized their slim lead would have to be enough. Their passion increased. Their skating accelerated.

And when the Capitals pulled their goalie, it was a couple minutes of all-out war, Washington trying desperately to slap anything on net, Osgood and company keeping them at bay. There were near misses and close shots and the kind of screams you normally hear in horror movies.

But in the end, the Wings heard the horn sound to put a 1-0 series lead in their pocket.

"I didn't think I had a very good game as coach," Scotty Bowman said. "We were mixed up early in the game, and some line combinations were off out there."

Whoa. Did you ever think you'd hear Scotty say that?

Then again, whoever thought you'd have to tell folks from Washington to take more shots?

In the middle of the game, the Caps went 15 minutes without recording a shot. When they finally got one, it was high and gloved by Osgood.

Of course, all naps have to end, and the Caps woke up with a Richard Zednick slapper that ended Osgood's shutout streak at 4⅔ periods.

"I don't think we were dominated out there by any means," Caps coach Ron Wilson said.

"We read the papers. We were supposed to get blasted out of here 5-0 or 6-0. It didn't happen."

It's true. Washington came

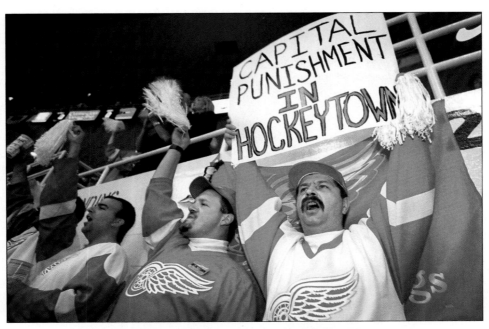

The verdict was in as far as Gary Ramey, right, of Taylor and
Bob Scott, center, of Inkster were concerned.

out with a bit more fire than Detroit. But for the most part, the first 15 minutes were little more than introductory, the hockey equivalent of a wine-and-cheese soiree, quiet, nothing controversial, the distant echo of a yawn.

Then came Detroit's secret weapon, that master of offense, Joey (Money) Kocur, who took a centering pass from Doug Brown and plunked it past Olaf Kolzig.

Kocur has a nice little streak going. He scored in the first game of last year's finals. He scored in the first game of this year's playoffs. And he scored in the first game of this year's finals.

Never mind that he barely scores in between. The goal unleashed a flood of noise that seemed to wash over the Wings and loosen their joints.

They skated more freely, more confidently, and just over two minutes later, Steve Yzerman sent a pass to Nick Lidstrom in his favorite spot, center ice, inside the blue line, and Lidstrom slapped a shot past a slightly screened Kolzig for goal No. 2.

But that would be it for the Detroit scoring. The rest would be their defense. It would be enough.

"I don't mind that there weren't a lot of shots," said Osgood, after winning his first career finals start. "If they don't have a lot of shots, it means they can't score."

Good point.

Caps Capped.

Game 1 Summary

Red Wings 2, Capitals 1

Washington	0	1	0 —	1
Detroit	2	0	0 —	2

First period
Detroit, Kocur 4 (Brown, Holmstrom), 14:04
Detroit, Lidstrom 6 (Yzerman, Holmstrom), 16:18

Second period
Washington, Zednik 7 (Nikolishin, Bondra), 15:57

Penalties
1st: Lapointe, Det (tripping), 4:21; Tinordi, Was (interference), 17:22.
2nd: Detroit bench, served by Kozlov (too many men), 5:48; Yzerman, Det (slashing), 8:51; Simon, Was (roughing), 18:06. **3rd:** Nikolishin, Was (interference), :48; Kocur, Det (roughing), 4:19.

Shots: Washington 6-4-7—17; Detroit 10-9-12—31. **Power plays:** Washington 0 of 4; Detroit 0 of 3. **Goalies:** Washington, Kolzig (12-6); Detroit, Osgood (13-6). **A:** 19,983. **Referee:** Bill McCreary. **Linesmen:** Ray Scapinello, Dan Schachte.

Doug Brown's goal with 4:14 left in regulation tied the game at 4 and erased the Wings' second two-goal deficit.

The comeback kids

*Thursday, June 11, 1998 —
Somewhere along the line, all
champions are tested. The Red Wings'
test would come in Game 2.*

By Jason La Canfora

Kris Draper circled behind the Washington net.
   The puck was in the right corner, where Martin Lapointe grabbed it. By now, Draper was alone in front of the net, while Capitals goalie Olaf Kolzig hugged the opposite post.

The grinder finished the feed with ease. After 93 shots — 60 directed at Kolzig — and 75:24 of hockey, the Red Wings capped a miraculous comeback and knocked off the Caps, 5-4, in overtime at Joe Louis Arena.
   "This is it," Draper said. "This is my biggest goal. This is what you dream about as a little kid playing ball hockey

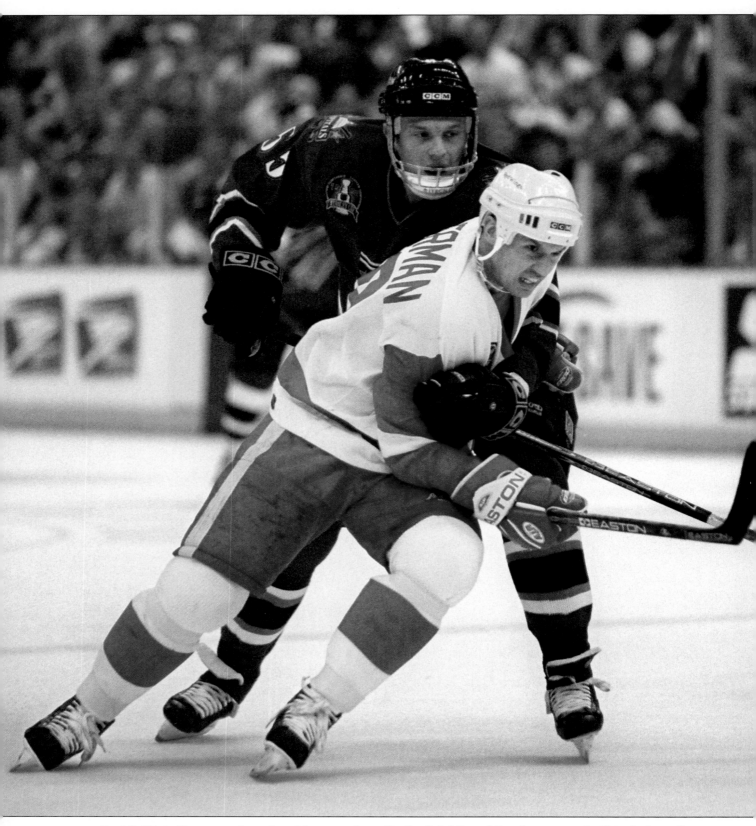

Captain Steve Yzerman, above, breaking away from the Capitals' Sergei Gonchar, was relentless in Game 2. He scored the Wings' first goal and narrowed the gap to 3-2 with a shorthanded tally in the third period.

THE FINALS

Joey Kocur got a right-handed facial from Washington's Esa Tikkanen as a linesman tried to separate them.

as the clock is counting down.

"The guys were saying (before OT) that the hero was going to be in this dressing room. . . . I think if you threw all the names in a hat, mine would have been the last one you pulled out. But I'll take it."

The celebration began in the third period and never stopped. The Wings scored three times in about nine minutes, pumping 20 shots at Kolzig.

It was the kind of comeback that defines championship teams and marks a dynasty. Two-goal deficits. Time winding down. The Stanley Cup finals. A building so loud you could taste the applause.

"I told them at the end of the third period, we have to attack for sure," coach Scotty Bowman said. "But we have to do it smart."

The Wings came into the third trailing, 3-1 — after yielding three goals in the second — and left it looking like an unstoppable machine, a group that could score whenever it was needed most, as if willing the puck into the goal.

The comeback started with the Captain, Steve Yzerman, who netted his first two-goal playoff game since 1996. Once, long ago in the first period, he

gave Detroit a 1-0 lead, poking a loose puck over the line.

In the third, he broke in short-handed on a two-on-one, held the puck for what seemed an eternity, making Kolzig and Sergei Gonchar think pass, then beat the goalie with a wrist shot at 6:37.

The Caps responded 28 seconds later, when Joe Juneau hammered a one-timer past Chris Osgood.

Down two goals again, the reins were off; the Wings played wide-open hockey, as run-and-gun as it gets. And Esa Tikkanen almost burned them on a breakaway, but slid the puck past an open net.

Igor Larionov won a face-off; Lapointe reached the loose puck and sent it in with 11:52 left for his eighth goal, cutting the deficit to 4-3.

Then, with 4:14 left in regulation, Doug Brown dashed in on Kolzig and sent the Wings' 44th shot over his shoulder, tying the game at 4.

The building was electric.

Only one sound would top that, the ecstasy of the overtime winner that erased the memory of a nightmare second period.

Washington had survived another shaky first period, regrouped at

Game 2 Summary

Red Wings 5, Capitals 4 (OT)

Washington	0	3	1	0	— 4
Detroit	1	0	3	1	— 5

First period
Detroit, Yzerman 5 (Holmstrom, Lidstrom), 7:49

Second period
Washington, Bondra 7 (Nikolishin, J.Brown), 1:51
Washington, Simon 1 (J.Brown), 6:11
Washington, Oates 6 (Juneau, Johansson), 11:03

Third period
Detroit, Yzerman 6 (Fetisov, McCarty), 6:37 (sh)
Washington, Juneau 7 (Gonchar, Bellows), 7:05 (pp)
Detroit, Lapointe 8 (Larionov, Fetisov), 8:08
Detroit, D.Brown 2, 15:46

Overtime
Detroit, Draper 1 (Lapointe, Shanahan), 15:24

Penalties
1st: Reekie, Was (holding), 13:05; Bondra, Was (hooking), 15:22. **2nd:** Maltby, Det (high-sticking), 3:09; Zednik, Was (hooking), 7:12; Simon, Was (roughing), 14:11; Osgood, Det, served by Kocur (unsportsmanlike conduct), 14:11; Maltby (slashing), 16:20. **3rd:** Lidstrom, Det (interference), 6:23; Zednik, Was (cross-checking), 10:18; Lapointe, Det (interference), 11:40. **OT:** Tikkanen, Was (roughing), 5:24; Kocur, Det (roughing), 5:24.

Shots: Washington 8-15-7-3—33; Detroit 14-14-20-12—60. **Power plays:** Washington 1 of 4; Detroit 0 of 4. **Goalies:** Washington, Kolzig (12-7); Detroit, Osgood 14-6 (33-29). **A:** 19,983. **Referee:** Don Koharski. **Linesmen:** Kevin Collins, Gord Broseker.

Kris Draper's overtime shot got past "Olie the Goalie" ...

... and started a wild Joe Louis celebration with Draper the center of attention.

Olie the Goalie

Sixty shots? Just another night's work for Washington's Olaf Kolzig.

Olie the Goalie faced 60 Red Wings shots — 48 in regulation and 20 in the third period alone — in the 5-4 overtime loss in Game 2.

"That's what I get paid for," he said. "I enjoy it. It keeps me in the game. I just go out there and try to give the guys a chance to win — whether it's 15 shots or 50 shots."

He had been doing it throughout the playoffs, facing an average of 34 shots in the first three rounds. By contrast, Chris Osgood had faced an average of 27.

Basically, Kolzig was the reason the Capitals were playing for the Stanley Cup.

Kolzig entered the finals leading the league in save percentage (.946), goals-against average (1.71), shutouts (4), minutes played (1,157), shots faced (608) and saves made (575).

"Godzilla gives us a chance to win," teammate Peter Bondra said. "He is Godzilla. He's a monster. He's the best goalie right now — in the whole league."

The 6-foot-3, 225-pound Kolzig was an overnight sensation with the Caps — after five seasons as a part-timer and never accumulating more than eight victories in a season.

Then came this season. Starter Bill Ranford was hurt, and Kolzig, 28, figured he'd better make a run at the No. 1 job before it was too late. He won — and won and won.

His final tally for the season was a 33-18-10 record, 2.20 goals-against and .920 save percentage.

"I've exceeded all my expectations and a lot of people's expectations," Kolzig said. "I've always believed that I could be an effective goaltender, that I could be a starting goalie, but it was just a matter of time before I was going to say to myself, 'It's time to go for it.'

"I got confidence in winning, then my play was a lot better, and then I started winning games that I shouldn't have, and it snowballed from there into a heck of a season."

By Helene St. James and Nicholas J. Cotsonika

intermission and returned a new team.

The game seemed to turn on a fluke play, when Peter Bondra chased down a long clearing pass that most Wings had given up on, thinking it was icing or a two-line pass.

It was neither — officials said Andrei Nikolishin tipped the pass in the neutral zone — and Bondra fired a bad-angle shot past a stunned Osgood for a 1-1 tie just 1:51 into the second period.

Within nine minutes, Chris Simon and Adam Oates also had scored for the rejuvenated Caps. They had three

goals on six shots and led, 3-1, with nine minutes left in the period.

The Wings had come unglued — but only temporarily.

By the time Draper scored, all the pieces were back in place, and Detroit had its first 2-0 series lead of the playoffs.

"It figures that it would be Drapes to get the winner," Lapointe said. "It seems like it's always somebody different who steps up and contributes.

"And we definitely needed a lot to come back tonight."

Lobbying for a sweep

Saturday, June 13, 1998 — The Red Wings couldn't forget what that date meant to them; it was the anniversary of the limousine crash. But they came to Washington with a job to do — and they did it.

By Jason La Canfora

They huddled around a plastic Stanley Cup and chanted hours before game time.

Hordes of Red Wings fans flooded the F Street entrance to the MCI Center, screaming "Oz-zie, Oz-zie." They could have saluted anyone, "Ste-vie, Ste-vie" or "Ser-gei, Ser-gei," but maybe they knew something.

As cars covered in Wings flags raced up the street with horns honking, perhaps they knew the goalie would be the hero in Game 3 of the Stanley Cup finals.

Osgood made 17 saves, Sergei Fedorov scored the game winner with 4:51 left, and the Wings didn't disappoint their traveling contingent, sneaking by Washington, 2-1, for a commanding 3-0 series lead, one victory from their second straight Cup.

"He played tremendously," Nick Lidstrom said of Osgood. "We had to kill off almost three penalties in a row, and he was really standing on his head and making some key saves. He made some unbelievable glove saves. He made some really big-time saves tonight."

Thousands of Michiganders came to the District of Columbia for the game, yelling and hollering choruses of "Let's Go, Wings." The game sounded as if it was played in Detroit, not hundreds of miles away.

And 35 seconds into the game, they had something to cheer about.

Steve Yzerman plowed down the left wing with the puck, stormed through the crease, and goalie Olaf Kolzig couldn't handle the rush. The puck squirmed out from beneath him, and Tomas Holmstrom punched it in for his seventh goal.

The assist was the Captain's NHL-

Tomas Holmstrom, who scored just 35 seconds into the game when he banged a rebound past Olaf Kolzig, skates toward Steve Yzerman, whose fierce rush started the play.

leading 24th point, setting a new personal high and tying Fedorov's team record.

"I've never seen him this way game-in and game-out at both ends of the ice," Joey Kocur said of Yzerman. "I was fortunate enough to play with him when he was incredible offensively, but now he's given up a little of that offensive talent and played the way Scotty Bowman wants him to play."

Associate coach Barry Smith agreed: "He's been the best player in the NHL since the Olympics. He's always raised his game for the playoffs, but now it's so consistently high. It's up there all the time. It's never coming down."

The Wings outshot the Caps, 13-1, in the first period. Since 1968, only one other team had been held to one shot in a period in the finals, and that was Detroit in the third period of Game 4 at New Jersey in 1995.

Despite the dominance, despite three power plays, despite Slava Kozlov's breakaway chance that was denied by Kolzig, Washington trailed only 1-0. And the Caps came out more determined in the second period.

"We ran into an opponent that was really upset about their first period," Smith said. "That six minutes of penalty kill really wore down our top six

Out of nowhere

Who was this guy, this Tomas Holmstrom?

He assisted on both Red Wings goals in Game 1 of the finals and their first in Game 2. He scored 35 seconds into Game 3 for a 1-0 lead that lasted into the third period.

That gave Holmstrom — who scored five goals and 22 points in the regular season — seven goals and 18 points in the playoffs.

How did the Wings find him?

Credit Hakan Andersson, the team's European scouting director. He spotted Holmstrom at Sweden's tryouts for the 1991 world junior hockey championships.

Holmstrom was 18 then, 5-feet-10 and 165 pounds. Andersson jotted down a few notes ("Love his attitude, way too small").

Later Andersson began hearing that this kid from up north — Holmstrom came from Pieta, a town of about 49,000 near the Arctic Circle — had grown.

The winger was now 6-feet and 210 pounds, his skating had improved some, and he was playing adrenaline-rush hockey.

"His coach told me, 'You better see him play — you better get up here,' " Andersson said. "You know, his nickname is the Demolition Man, and he was hitting people a lot more than he does now.

"In his second-to-last year in Sweden, his coach said it must have been 10 to 15 guys carried off the ice that year that Tomas hit."

Holmstrom couldn't skate well, and he was already 21 with what appeared to be a limited upside. But when the Wings' ninth pick came up in the June 1994 draft, Andersson persuaded them to gamble on Holmstrom with the 257th selection.

Holmstrom played two more seasons in Sweden's Elite League, spent six games in Adirondack in 1996-97, and has been in Detroit ever since.

"I get over here, and everything is flying by me," Holmstrom said. "It goes so fast, you don't know what day it is. Everything's going so fast. I'm having a really great time."

By Jason La Canfora

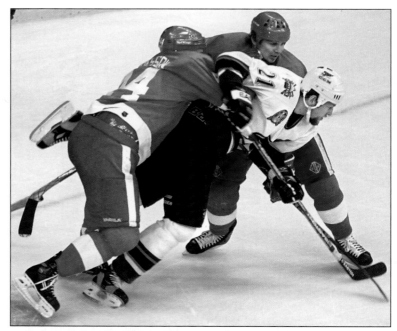

Anders Eriksson, left, and Igor Larionov veto the passage of the Capitals' Jeff Toms during the second period.

forwards. It hurt us and gave them a little more momentum."

But no goals, thanks to Osgood.

Early in the period, Jeff Toms shot through traffic, and the puck slithered through, but Osgood dove back and gloved it near the goal line.

"Oz-zie, Oz-zie." For 15 seconds it felt just like Joe Louis Arena.

The Caps drew a standing ovation on their next power play but still no goals. Osgood robbed Brian Bellows with a two-pad slide and gloved down a cross-ice feed with Adam Oates alone at the other post.

He caught a piece of an Oates slap shot, and it trickled wide. Joe Juneau and Phil Housley sent blasts just wide as well, and the arena was alive, as was the home team.

It got worse.

Richard Zednik fed sniper Peter Bondra for a point-blank one-timer, but Osgood was there. Suddenly, he was bailing out his team.

"Ozzie played great for us," Bob Rouse said. "He was terrific when we needed him."

Osgood stoned Bondra on a two-on-one with less than two minutes left in the period, whipping up his glove hand to snare the shot.

Oates and Bondra challenged in the opening minutes of the third period. They were stopped again, but they never

Chris Osgood, who had 17 saves on the night, prompted rowdy chants of "Oz-zie, Oz-zie" from the considerable Red Wings'
contingent in the crowd. He still had a shutout working at the start of the third period.

Kirk Maltby went airborne to pressure Washington's Chris Simon as the two fought for the puck in the first period, which ended with the Red Wings leading, 1-0.

stopped coming.

Oates rushed on goal midway through the period. Kirk Maltby slid into the crease to block the puck, and, as he and Osgood tried to cover it, Bellows crashed the net and slammed it home.

The Wings had let another lead slip away, failing to build on it and take advantage of frequent chances. They were tied at 1 with 9:25 left in regulation. Neither team was opening up much. Overtime seemed a certainty.

In one moment, one Fedorov move, all of that changed.

He darted down the right wing, slipped into neutral, cut inside on defenseman Calle Johansson and fired back to the near post, beating Kolzig high to his glove side with 4:51 to play. Fedorov had scored just his second goal in the last 11 games at the most opportune time.

"That was a big-time goal from a big-time player," coach Scotty Bowman said.

A big, ugly octopus fell to the ice. Roars sprung up throughout the crowd. Soon, the pockets of Wings fans would sprinkle back to the streets, in their Winged Wheel sweaters and into their flag-waving cars.

This near-summer Washington night was theirs.

Game 3 Summary

Red Wings 2, Capitals 1

Detroit	1	0	1 — 2
Washington	0	0	1 — 1

First Period
Detroit, Holmstrom 7 (Yzerman, McCarty), :35

Third period
Washington, Bellows 5 (Oates, Juneau), 10:35 (pp)
Detroit, Fedorov 10 (D.Brown, Fetisov), 15:09

Penalties
  1st: Simon, Was (slashing), 2:48; Hunter, Was (charging), 8:10; Housley, Was (elbowing), 12:29; Holmstrom, Det (goalie interference), 13:11; Lapointe, Det (interference), 17:01. **2nd:** Krygier, Was (roughing), 2:05; Eriksson, Det (holding), 7:29; Larionov, Det (tripping), 10:17; Draper, Det (roughing), 15:23; Gonchar, Was (roughing), 15:23. **3rd:** Gonchar, Was (roughing), 5:50; McCarty, Det (tripping), 9:22.

  Shots: Detroit 13-11-10—34; Washington 1-12-5—18. **Power plays:** Detroit 0 of 5; Washington 1 of 5. **Goalies:** Detroit, Osgood (15-6); Washington, Kolzig (12-8). **A:** 19,740. **Referee:** Terry Gregson. **Linesmen:** Ray Scapinello, Dan Schachte.

Amid the glory, a sad anniversary

When the final horn sounded, Sergei Fedorov picked up the game puck as a souvenir for Vladimir Konstantinov or Sergei Mnatsakanov.

"I am crying my eyes right now because I got the puck," Fedorov said. "First I am going to keep it a while and decide what I am going to do.

"Just for the appreciation of what Vladdie and Sergei did for this team; just show them and maybe one would like to keep it."

Scotty Bowman put the victory, which gave the Wings a 3-0 lead over Washington in the Stanley Cup finals, in perspective.

"This pales in importance to what those two warriors that are still recovering have to face," Bowman said.

A year ago to the night, Slava Fetisov, Konstantinov and Mnatsakanov were injured in the fateful limousine accident.

Fetisov came back to play, but Konstantinov and Mnatsakanov weren't so fortunate.

"I wish we didn't have to play this night, but they chose this date," said Fetisov, who assisted on the winning goal. "There is a lot of emotion and memories. Scotty mentioned before the game that we have to play this for the boys.

"All these pictures in the last moments before the crash . . . I try to stay away but you can't. It's the kind of thing you want to forget, but you're never going to forget what happened.

"I called to Vladimir before the game, to ask him what he thinks. I asked him if he was going to watch the game and he said, 'Yes, I'm going to watch the game.' He wished us good luck."

The subject came up in in the dressing room before the game.

"Each player kind of had 20 seconds of silence to think about those guys and pray for them," Igor Larionov said. "I think it helped us to be more united as a team to play our best hockey."

"Just before we went out onto the ice," Martin Lapointe said, "Scotty reminded us to give our maximum effort for them.

"Scotty said that he would give up all of his Stanley Cup championship rings if the two of them could be standing in this locker room with us today. It was pretty inspiring."

As the date approached, the Wings were forced to balance some pretty heavy emotions, for their friends and for their task at hand.

"We feel very, very much for Vladdie and Sergei," Fedorov said. "We always say that first we get the job done and then we come back and hug them and shake their hands.

"It's sad thing what happened, but we have to move on. If we had stuck with

Sergei Fedorov, who scored the winning goal in Game 3, raced to snag the puck when the final horn sounded. He wanted it for his friends, Vladimir Konstantinov and Sergei Mnatsakanov, injured a year before to the day in the limousine accident.

feeling angry, it would be much, much tougher to play for each of us.

"But everybody took that responsibility that Vladdie and Sergei cannot be with us every time, but we remember them and we always will."

While their hearts were filled with love and hope for Konstantinov and Mnatsakanov, some Wings said they harbored no bitterness for the limousine driver, Richard Gnida.

Gnida was due to be released the next week after serving seven months of a nine-month sentence for driving on a suspended license. He still had 200 hours of community service to perform with victims of brain injuries.

"I think he paid a price and he still will throughout his life," Fedorov said. "Because what he did will always stick with him. Just like it will stick with us throughout our lives."

Bob Rouse agreed: "You can look at how unfair it was, but you can't dwell on that. I don't think it's productive for anybody to keep anger in them.

"Now is a time to look forward and try and do your best to support their families, and, if anything, try to learn from this situation — realize that life is very fragile, so enjoy the moment."

By Helene St. James and Drew Sharp

A Cup for Vladdie and Sergei

By Jason La Canfora

He was wheeled through the concourse with 8½ minutes left in the season, no longer able to play, no longer able to walk on his own.

His Red Wings teammates had a second consecutive Stanley Cup well in hand. A sweep of the Washington Capitals was certain.

It was time for Vladimir Konstantinov to celebrate.

He was wheeled onto the ice, and trainer John Wharton rushed to greet him. The Wings were shaking hands with the Capitals, the series wrapped up with a 4-1 victory.

"Vlad-die! Vlad-die! Vlad-die!"

The MCI Center roared its salute, and the Wings gathered around their fallen teammate, the fearless leader who was a demon on the ice for them one year ago, before he nearly died in a limo accident last June.

Konstantinov pulled a cigar to his mouth and raised his index finger. He and his buddies were indeed No. 1 again.

Captain Steve Yzerman, the Conn Smythe Trophy winner as playoff MVP, raised the Cup first, as he did last year, then put it on Konstantinov's lap. Everyone gathered around for a group photo, Vladdie sporting his 1998 Stanley Cup champions cap.

"This is Vladdie's Cup," Igor Larionov said. "I know he could enjoy it. He understood what was going on. He'll come back and walk again on his own. He'll lead a normal life. I know it."

Wharton said, "This Cup wasn't for Vladdie and Sergei, it was because of them."

The ninth Stanley Cup in the Wings' 72-year history belongs to Konstantinov and

The Wings struck first on Doug Brown's power-play goal at 10:30 of the first period. Brown, celebrating with Tomas Holmstrom, left, and Sergei Fedorov, scored again on a power play at 1:32 of the third period.

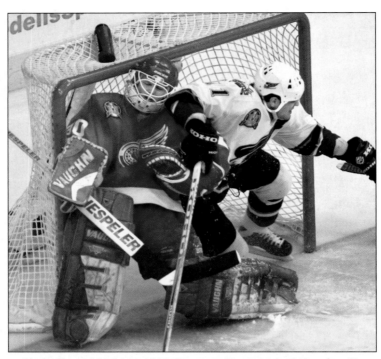

Chris Osgood had one of his best performances of the playoffs in Game 4, stopping 30 shots and Esa Tikkanen in the second period. Tikkanen was called for goalie interference, and Larry Murphy scored 44 seconds later.

Sergei Mnatsakanov as much as anyone. The former all-star defenseman and the massage therapist were robbed of their livelihoods, and nearly their lives, on June 13, 1997.

But no one can take June 16, 1998, away.

The Wings became the first team to repeat since Pittsburgh in 1991-92 and the fifth team to sweep consecutive finals.

Yzerman tied Sergei Fedorov's team playoff records with 24 points and 18 assists and displayed unparalleled guts and passion every night.

Scotty Bowman tied Toe Blake's record with his eighth Stanley Cup behind the bench.

Chris Osgood proved he was strong enough to take the team to the Cup, erasing memories of last year's playoff MVP Mike Vernon.

Nick Lidstrom demonstrated again why he is perhaps the best defenseman in the world.

And everyone else, from Joey Kocur to Kris Draper to Tomas Holmstrom, provided huge goals in between.

But this Cup was a tribute to Konstantinov, the rugged defenseman, once perhaps the best in the world, who now needs help walking and feeding himself.

This Cup was a tribute to Mnatsakanov, who will never walk again. He receives care now, no longer a caregiver.

Konstantinov and his wife, Irina, flew to Washington for the game. His wheelchair was stationed in the second level, behind the goal the Wings attacked in the first and third periods. There he sat with Irina, behind a sign that read "WE BELIEVE, YOU BELIEVE" in section 116, so close to the number he wore for Detroit.

"I don't think any of the guys didn't recognize when he first appeared there," Wharton said. "We all knew immediately when he was first present, and I think we built off that moment. It was kind of a silent

When Martin Lapointe scored the Wings' second goal, his ninth of the playoffs, it gave Detroit some breathing room. But the Capitals weren't quite finished. Brian Bellows cut the lead to 2-1 when he scored Washington's only goal five minutes later.

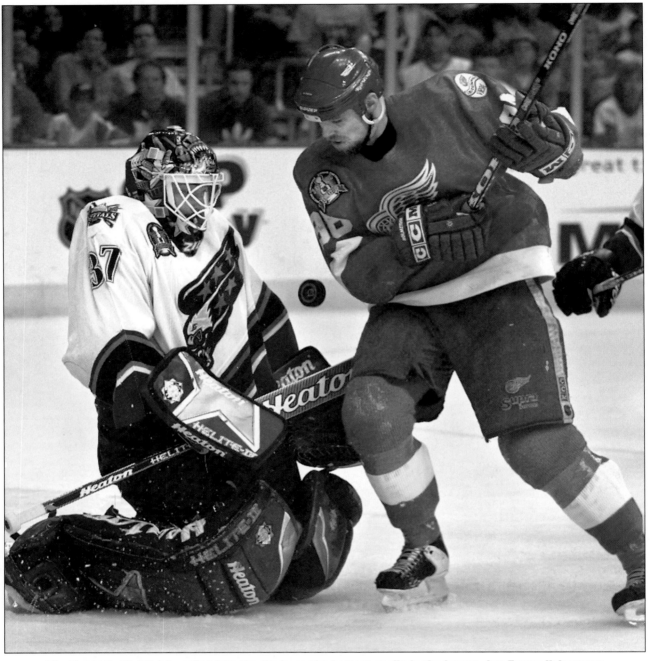

Washington's Olaf Kolzig rolled into the finals as the hottest goalie in the league, but Tomas Holmstrom and the Wings were too hot to handle. They peppered him with 38 shots in the Cup-clincher.

acknowledgement."

Wharton said he regretted that Mnatsakanov didn't make the trip; the two spent countless hours together behind the bench and in the training room.

"I really miss Sergei," Wharton said. "I really, really wish he could have been here. But we talked about it before the game and how he wants to be at the parade. And that would be the most proud moment of my career, to be able to share a vehicle with him at the parade. To do that

would be awesome."

The Wings began slowly, as Washington attacked. Then, in a matter of minutes, the home team dissolved into the Caps we came to know in the series.

They struggled, unable or

"It felt great when everyone stands up and cheers.
Vladdie deserves that. We could not do this without Vladdie.
We miss him on the ice for so long. It was good to see him back."

Slava Kozlov
Red Wings forward

There weren't many dry eyes in Hockeytown when Vladimir Konstantinov was shown during Game 4 in Washington. Nicole Playmaker, 16, of Harrison Township and Bill Sheridan of Macomb cheered on the Wings at sold-out Joe Vision at Joe Louis Arena.

unwilling to shoot the puck. They generated no sustained offense. They didn't challenge. Didn't come close.

The Wings took 11 of 12 shots on goal in one eight-minute tear, and Osgood was at peace in his crease, isolated from the puck. The Wings fans in attendance — and there were thousands — roared with each near-miss.

Midway through the period, the guy who cemented the Game 3 victory set up Game 4's opening goal.

Fedorov skated the puck hard, turning, curling, spinning away from danger, and looking alertly cross-ice. There he found Doug Brown, threaded a pass to him, and Brown slammed it between goalie Olaf Kolzig and the near post.

The Red Wings led, 1-0, 10:30 into the game

Larry Murphy picked a good time to score his only goal of the finals, nipping Washington's comeback bid at 11:46 of the second period. His third goal of the playoffs gave the Wings a 3-1 lead.

Worth every penny

By Nicholas J. Cotsonika

If the desire to replace past pains with the greatest of hockey glories could be measured in speed, Sergei Fedorov was the hungriest player on the ice for some of the most important moments of the Stanley Cup finals.

When Fedorov was at his best, he was truly a man of the Motor City. His legs pumped like pistons. His heart, fueled by thoughts of Vladimir Konstantinov and Sergei Mnatsakanov, was an enormous engine of energy. His mind hoped he would be remembered for more than his sticker price.

"Deep inside, I always wanted to stay here and play," said a champagne-stained Fedorov, who as a holdout months before had declared he would never again play for the Wings.

"To be honest, I never thought I would, but I hoped I would," he said.

"I think about it, and Detroit is my second hometown. I came here from Russia only to play for the Red Wings, and I can never forget that I'm a hockey player here and I have to produce and play well."

The Wings' most talented player came through in the most trying of times — the elusive moments of eliminating a worthy opponent.

And, in the end, he held the Stanley Cup high, knowing he was an important contributor to the Wings' second straight finals sweep.

In Game 3, Fedorov raced all over the ice, collecting 13 shots, and scored the winning goal — his league-leading 10th — in a tense third period. In Game 4, he flew again, smacking into anyone he could find and creating offense as only he can. He set up two of the Wings' goals.

He said his performance — but more important, his effort — was his personal demonstration that magic can mean more than money.

After he held out for the season's first 59 games and signed an offer sheet with the Carolina Hurricanes, saying he would not play in Detroit again, coach Scotty Bowman said the Wings decided they couldn't do without him.

They matched the Hurricanes' $38-million offer and kept Fedorov, but many viewed his return to the team with

Sergei Fedorov, who missed 59 regular-season games in a contract hold-out, devoted his run in the finals to winning back Red Wings fans. "Some people got mad because of what happened," he said. "My challenge was to win some fans back. I wouldn't let anybody stop me."

cynical eyes.

To some, the push for a big contract indicated an absence of passion for the game. But Fedorov, who clinched a $12-million bonus in bulk when the Wings advanced to the Western Conference finals, made it his mission to change the opinion of fans in the finals.

"Some people got mad because of what happened," Fedorov said. "My challenge was to win some fans back. I really had a good chance to do that, and now we're back on top. Things worked out. I wouldn't let anybody stop me."

As the clock wound down in Washington, it was time to celebrate for, from left, Joey Kocur, Kris Draper, Steve Yzerman, Kirk Maltby and Tomas Holmstrom.

Some fans took to the air to celebrate the Wings' second consecutive Stanley Cup sweep, as more than 20,000 people packed Royal Oak's Main Street after Game 4.

with their first power-play goal of the series after 12 chances. The lead was small, but commanding: Detroit entered the game 12-1 when scoring first in the playoffs.

Then Martin Lapointe struck from the blue line, just 2:26 into the second period. Wings 2, Caps 0.

Irina Konstantinov jumped with glee, pumping her hands. She reached over to her husband, clenching his wrists and waving his arms in unbridled emotion.

A chant of "Vlad-die! Vlad-die!" sprung from the upper deck.

Caps forward Brian Bellows interrupted the display by banging in a rebound, making it 2-1 with 12 minutes left in the period.

It was a temporary disruption — very temporary.

Less than four minutes later, Larry Murphy, the former Capital booed derisively by the Washington fans, stood on the right face-off dot and beat Kolzig's glove hand, making it 3-1.

Irina bounced up and down, took off her white sweater and whipped it around her head ferociously. She high-fived the Wings fans one row in front of her. She could feel the victory.

Brown, with three goals and five points in the series, banged in Slava

Back where he belongs

By John Lowe

As soon as the Red Wings brought the Stanley Cup into their dressing room, they made sure Vladimir Konstantinov drank from it.

Kris Draper poured champagne into the Cup.

"You want a sip?" he asked.

And Konstantinov beamed, maybe even a little more brightly than he already was.

Draper and Chris Osgood carried the Cup to the corner where Konstantinov sat in a wheelchair. They slowly tilted it toward his mouth, making sure not to spill the bubbly.

Konstantinov smiled broadly.

And then he drank from the Cup.

Moments later, he smiled as Igor Larionov sang, "We are the champions, we are the champions."

The Queen song was one of the first things that brought a response from Konstantinov as he lay comatose in Beaumont Hospital after the limousine accident. It was played at Joe Louis Arena after the Wings beat Philadelphia for the 1997 Cup.

And on this night, although he didn't speak, Konstantinov seemed to understand fully that the Red Wings had won another Cup. His face was aglow. His eyes were bright as he looked around the room. He smiled often. He looked like a man watching his favorite show.

As soon as he was wheeled into the dressing room, defenseman Bob Rouse and trainer John Wharton presented him with a bottle of champagne. He took a sip.

Soon, Konstantinov was doused by flying champagne. He smiled.

The small dressing room was filled with players, their families, club officials and the media. But the Russian players made sure Konstantinov wasn't lost in the crowd. At least one was with him at all times.

"This is very emotional for us," Larionov said.

Slava Fetisov put his arm around Konstantinov. A moment later, Konstantinov poured champagne down Fetisov's throat. Then Fetisov returned the favor.

Konstantinov took his second drink from the Cup. Slava Kozlov came back for a photo with Larionov. Dmitri Mironov, little used in the playoffs, logged a lot of minutes at Konstantinov's side.

After about a half-hour, Konstantinov was wheeled out.

Vladimir Konstantinov drank up the celebration — and the champagne — in the locker room after the Wings clinched the Cup.

"It's too hot in here for him," someone said. Irina, Konstantinov's wife, had been concerned he was drinking too much champagne.

At one point, Konstantinov held up one finger for No. 1, two fingers for the second straight Cup, and — at someone's behest — three fingers for next year's goal, three Cups in a row.

And maybe then he will be back in the celebration, standing on his own feet.

Kris Draper gave two thumbs up for two Stanley Cups in two years. Celebrating with him were reserve goalie Kevin Hodson, center, Darren McCarty, right, and Doug Brown, front.

Kozlov's feed 1:32 into the third period. Irina cheered again, and the finals were all but over.

"Vlad-die! Vlad-die! Vlad-die!"

It was coming from everywhere.

Konstantinov acknowledged the thunderous applause by standing. This wasn't just Wings fans anymore, it was the entire arena. Flashbulbs popped from every angle.

Konstantinov was back where he belonged.

"It felt great when everyone stands up and cheers," Kozlov said. "Vladdie deserves that. We could not do this without Vladdie. We miss him on the

ice for so long. It was good to see him back."

For months the fallen comrades were away from the rink, away from their buddies, but they were never forgotten. Silently, a bond was formed as the Wings gathered in Beaumont Hospital last June. Silently, they promised to play through the heartache, become a better team for it and persevere despite the absence of their friends.

They would celebrate again with Vladdie and Sergei, and they would do it in grand style. Last summer, they got six days. Now they have a lifetime.

The smiles say it all. Above, Chris Osgood — helping Kris Draper tote the Cup —
erased any doubts some fans had about his ability to win a Stanley Cup.
Right, Scotty Bowman raises his eighth Cup, tying him with legendary
Montreal Canadiens coach Toe Blake.

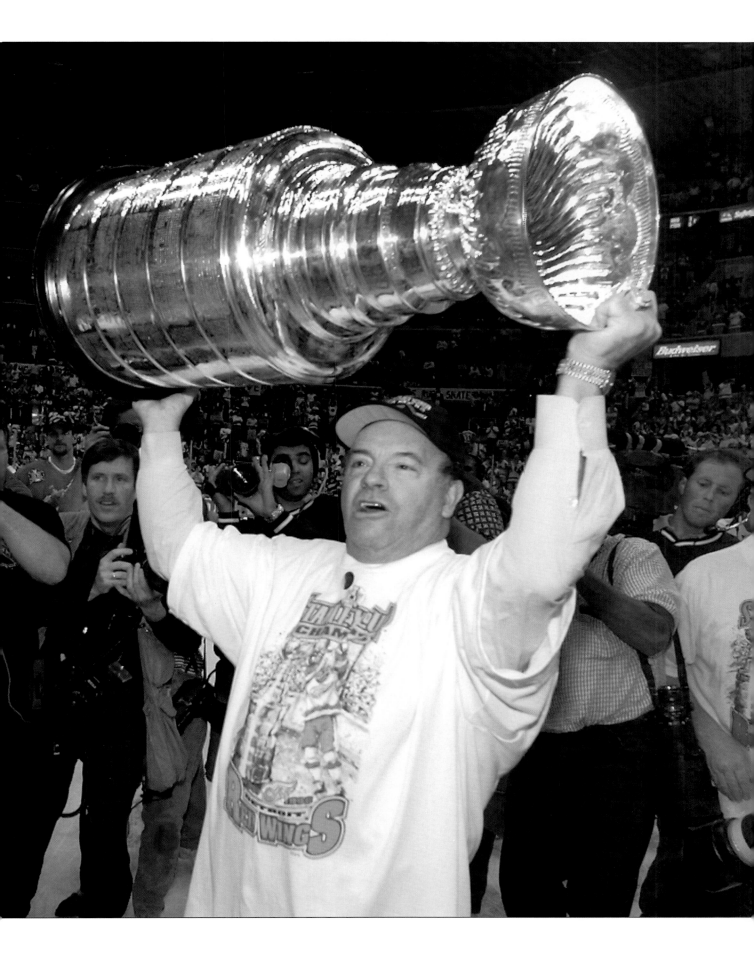

Our Captain

Conn Smythe validates Yzerman's status

By Drew Sharp

Steve Yzerman, who hoisted the Stanley Cup with a sense of relief a year ago, lifted it a second time, and in the process removed the final burden from his shoulders.

He proved last year that he could lead. This time, he proved he could star.

That rarefied air in which only the truly spectacular exist was exclusively his domain for a night — an occasion to bask in the glow of an outpouring of accolades.

But all Yzerman wanted to do was get out of his sweat- and champagne-soaked uniform, toss his Stanley Cup championship cap in the closet and concentrate on everything but hockey.

"I was getting sick and tired of wearing this thing," he said. "It's been a physically and emotionally draining season that just never seemed to end. As happy as I am to win, I'm equally happy that it's all over.

"I can lie around in the house, kick my feet up, watch some TV and just do nothing for a while."

Yzerman's evening turned even more poignant with two minutes remaining in the Red Wings' sweep. He thought he would give a vindicated Chris Osgood the ceremonial first handoff of the Stanley Cup.

But Brendan Shanahan and Igor Larionov approached Yzerman on the bench and asked whether he would present the Cup to Vladimir Konstantinov, who appeared in his Wings jersey for the first time since last year's Cup-clinching game against Philadelphia.

Yzerman had no idea his wounded teammate would participate in the on-ice celebration.

"It was an automatic decision," he said. "At this time a year ago, we still weren't sure if either Vladdie or Sergei were going to survive, so to have him on the ice with us was pretty significant."

From an emotional standpoint, this

Maybe now Conn Smythe winner Steve Yzerman will become a household name outside Detroit. "When I first came into the league, I don't think there were many people who could correctly spell or pronounce my name," he said.

championship was for Konstantinov and Sergei Mnatsakanov.

But from a competitive aspect, it was for the Captain.

Any questions that might have remained regarding his talent or toughness were answered decisively when he carried off the Conn Smythe Trophy as the playoffs' MVP.

As if there was any contest.

The 4-1 victory over Washington at the MCI Center marked the first time in the past two finals that Yzerman didn't register a point in a game. By the look on his face afterward, it didn't bother him.

"Yeah, there's a certain amount of gratification in having my name included on a trophy with so many great players," said Yzerman, who had six goals and a league-leading 24 points in the playoffs.

"When I first came into the league, I don't think there were many people who

could correctly spell or pronounce my name. Winning this award along with the Stanley Cup definitely is a nice stamp on my career."

New York Rangers general manager Neil Smith scouted Yzerman for the Wings in the 1983 draft. Few others have his special insight into Yzerman's evolution as a player.

"It's amazing he's still one of the best players in the whole playoffs at 33 years of age," Smith said. "He's been amazing. I think he's better now than he was earlier. He's a way more complete player, a better player."

But to appreciate where Yzerman is among the greats, you have to understand where he has been.

Smith recalled the critics when Team Canada selected Yzerman for the 1996 World Cup.

"They said he didn't have the makeup to really sacrifice himself in that kind of tournament," Smith said. "He was small, weak and not very good defensively. If he got hurt and couldn't play, no big deal. We don't need him. Who needs Steve Yzerman? He's never won anything. . . ."

Who needs Steve Yzerman?

Ask that question today, and a coach who just tied the record with eight Stanley Cup championships will raise his hand. So will 24 other players in a champagne-soaked dressing room and thousands of fans dancing in the streets of Detroit.

"Stevie's never really gotten the big recognition that the Gretzkys and Lemieuxs always got," teammate Martin Lapointe said. "We've always known what a great player and great leader he is, but winning two straight Stanley Cups would have to convince others of that as well."

The Wings fed off Yzerman's resolve. Nothing was going to stop them from succeeding again.

Yzerman wouldn't allow it.

"He's now considered the beacon of success," Smith said. "When you think of those who should be holding the Cup today, you think of Steve Yzerman."

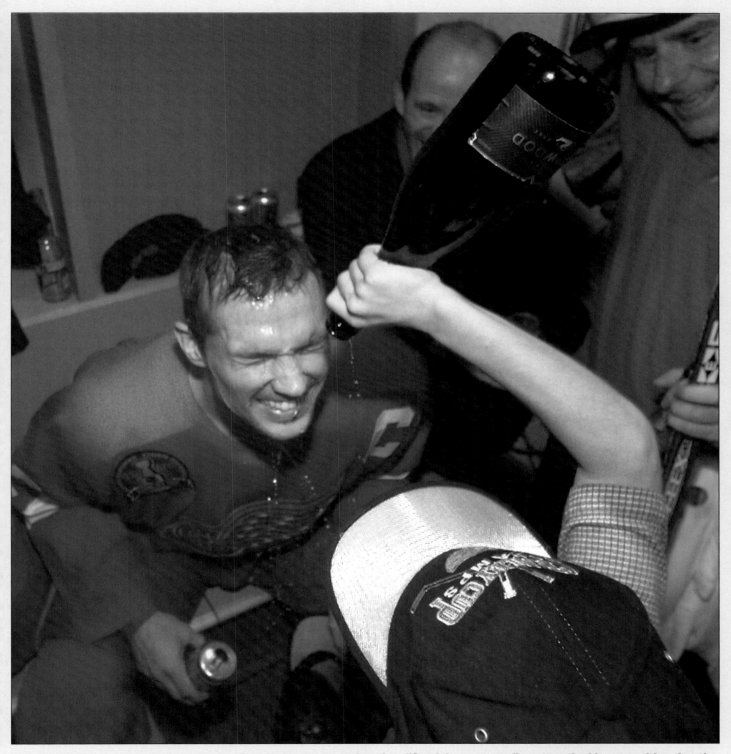

The Captain Steve Yzerman was showered with champagne and praise. "Stevie's never really gotten the big recognition that the Gretzkys and Lemieuxs always got," teammate Martin Lapointe said. "We've always known what a great player and great leader he is, but winning two straight Stanley Cups would have to convince others of that as well."

The Red Wings strike a Stanley Cup championship pose for the second straight year.

Regular-Season Stats

PLAYER	GP	G	A	PTS	+/-	PM	PP	SH	GW	SHT
Steve Yzerman	75	24	45	69	3	46	6	2	0	188
Nick Lidstrom	80	17	42	59	22	18	7	1	1	205
Brendan Shanahan	75	28	29	57	6	154	15	1	9	266
Slava Kozlov	80	25	27	52	14	46	6	0	1	221
Larry Murphy	82	11	41	52	35	37	2	1	2	129
Igor Larionov	69	8	39	47	14	40	3	0	2	93
Dmitri Mironov	77	8	35	43	-7	119	3	0	1	170
Doug Brown	80	19	23	42	17	12	6	1	5	145
Darren McCarty	71	15	22	37	0	157	5	1	2	166
Martin Lapointe	79	15	19	34	0	106	4	0	3	154
Brent Gilchrist	61	13	14	27	4	40	5	0	3	124
Kirk Maltby	65	14	9	23	11	89	2	1	3	106
Kris Draper	64	13	10	23	5	45	1	0	3	96
Tomas Holmstrom	57	5	17	22	6	44	1	0	1	48
Anders Eriksson **	66	7	14	21	21	32	1	0	2	91
Sergei Fedorov	21	6	11	17	10	25	2	0	2	68
Mathieu Dandenault	68	5	12	17	5	43	0	0	0	75
Slava Fetisov	58	2	12	14	5	72	0	0	1	55
Mike Knuble	53	7	6	13	2	16	0	0	0	54
Bob Rouse	71	1	11	12	-9	57	0	0	0	54
Joey Kocur	63	6	5	11	7	92	0	0	2	53
Aaron Ward	52	5	5	10	-1	47	0	0	1	47
Jamie Macoun	74	0	7	7	-17	65	0	0	0	78
Jamie Pushor*	54	2	5	7	2	71	0	0	0	43
Yan Golubovsky**	12	0	2	2	1	6	0	0	0	9
Darryl Laplante**	2	0	0	0	0	2	0	0	0	0
Norm Maracle**	4	0	0	0	0	0	0	0	0	0
Kevin Hodson	21	0	0	0	0	2	0	0	0	0
Chris Osgood	64	0	0	0	6	31	0	0	0	0

GOALIES	GP	MIN	AVG	W-L-T	SO	GA	SHT	SV%
Norm Maracle	4	178	2.02	2-0-1	0	6	63	.905
Chris Osgood	64	3,807	2.21	33-20-11	6	140	1,605	.913
Kevin Hodson	21	988	2.67	9-3-3	2	44	444	.901
TEAM	**82**	**4,995**	**2.35**	**44-23-15**	**9**	**196**	**2,118**	**.907**

Playoffs Stats

PLAYER	GP	G	A	PTS	+/-	PM
Steve Yzerman	22	6	18	24	10	22
Sergei Fedorov	22	10	10	20	0	12
Tomas Holmstrom	22	7	12	19	9	16
Nick Lidstrom	22	6	13	19	12	8
Martin Lapointe	21	9	6	15	6	20
Larry Murphy	22	3	12	15	12	2
Slava Kozlov	22	6	8	14	4	10
Igor Larionov	22	3	10	13	5	12
Darren McCarty	22	3	8	11	9	34
Brendan Shanahan	20	5	4	9	5	22
Doug Brown	9	4	2	6	-1	0
Anders Eriksson **	18	0	5	5	7	16
Joe Kocur	18	4	0	4	-3	30
Kirk Maltby	22	3	1	4	2	30
Jamie Macoun	22	2	2	4	3	18
Kris Draper	19	1	3	4	4	12
Brent Gilchrist	15	2	1	3	2	12
Dmitri Mironov	7	0	3	3	1	14
Slava Fetisov	21	0	3	3	4	10
Bob Rouse	22	0	3	3	2	16
Mathieu Dandenault	3	1	0	1	-2	0
Mike Knuble	3	0	1	1	0	0
Chris Osgood	22	0	1	1	0	12
Kevin Hodson	1	0	0	0	0	0

GOALIES	GP	MIN	AVG	W- L	SO	GA	SHT
Kevin Hodson	1	1	0.00	0- 0	0	0	0
Chris Osgood	22	1361	2.12	16- 6	2	48	588
TEAM	**22**	**1367**	**2.15**	**16- 6**	**2**	**49**	**589**

*Traded during season; **rookies; +/- — plus-minus rating (a plus is added for being on the ice when a goal is scored for a player's team in a full-strength situation; a minus is added for being on the ice when an opponent's goal is scored in a full-strength situation); PM — penalty minutes; PP — power play goals; SH — shorthanded goals; GW — game-winning goals; SHT — shots on goal.

Photographers

- **William Archie:** Pages 11 (top), 78 (top), 80 (left), 95, 96, 108.

- **Kirthmon F. Dozier:** Pages 1, 8 (bottom), 14, 24, 39, 41, 44 (top), 45, 49, 54, 57 (right), 61, 62 (bottom), 63, 64, 65, 66, 67, 69, 71, 85, 86, 88 (bottom), 91, 98, 102.

- **Kim Kim Foster:** Page 60.

- **David P. Gilkey:** Pages 10, 25 (right), 28.

- **Julian H. Gonzalez:** Pages 9 (fireworks), 20, 22-23, 25 (left), 26 (both), 29, 34, 35 (bottom), 36, 40, 43, 46 (bottom), 47, 48, 50, 52, 53, 55, 56, 57 (left), 58 (both), 59, 68, 70, 72 (bottom), 73 (bottom), 74, 76, 77, 78 (bottom), 79, 80 (right), 81, 82, 89, 90, 92, 93, 97, 100, 101, 104 (both), 106, 107, 109, 110, 112.

- **Richard Lee:** Page 11 (middle).

- **Pauline Lubens:** Page 99.

- **Rick Nease:** Page 75 illustration.

- **Craig Porter:** Pages 4-5, 7, 38.

- **Mary Schroeder:** Pages 13, 21, 32 (both), 33, 62 (top).

- **Gabriel B. Tait:** Pages 6, 8 (top), 12, 15, 44 (bottom), 46 (top), 72 (top), 73 (top), 83, 84, 87, 88 (top), 105.

- **Nico Toutenhoofd:** Page 103.

- **Special to the Free Press:** Ed Opp, Page 18.

- **Associated Press:** Tom Pidgeon, Page 27; Chuck Stoody, Page 30.

- **Allsport:** Ezra O. Shaw, Pages 16-17.; Al Bello, Page 35 (top); Todd Warsaw, Page 35 (middle); Doug Pensinger, Page 37.

Slava Fetisov, right, and the rest of the Wings made sure Vladimir Konstantinov knew
he would always be a part of the team. They Believed!